AMBIGUITIES IN
LITERATURE AND FILM

AMBIGUITIES IN
LITERATURE AND FILM

Selected Papers from the Seventh Annual
Florida State University Conference on
Literature and Film

Edited by Hans P. Braendlin

UNIVERSITY PRESSES OF FLORIDA

THE FLORIDA STATE UNIVERSITY PRESS
TALLAHASSEE

UNIVERSITY PRESSES OF FLORIDA is the central agency for scholarly publishing of the State of Florida's university system, producing books selected for publication by the faculty editorial committees of Florida's nine public universities: Florida A&M University (Tallahassee), Florida Atlantic University (Boca Raton), Florida International University (Miami), Florida State University (Tallahassee), University of Central Florida (Orlando), University of Florida (Gainesville), University of North Florida (Jacksonville), University of South Florida (Tampa), University of West Florida (Pensacola).

ORDERS for books published by all member presses of University Presses of Florida should be addressed to University Presses of Florida, 15 NW 15th Street, Gainesville, FL 32603.

Library of Congress Cataloging-in-Publication Data
Florida State University Conference on Literature and
        Film (7th : 1982)
        Ambiguities in literature and film: selected papers from the Seventh Annual Florida State University Conference on Literature and Film / edited by Hans Braendlin.

  Includes bibliographies.
  ISBN 0-8130-0893-x (alk. paper) : $12.00
  1. Ambiguity in literature—Congresses. 2. Ambiguity in motion pictures—Congresses. 3. Literature, Modern—20th century—History and criticism—Congresses. 4. Motion pictures—Congresses.
I. Braendlin, Hans. II. Title.
PN56.A55F55 1987
809—dc 19   87–31614 CIP

CONTENTS

ACKNOWLEDGMENTS

This volume presents a selection of papers from the Seventh Annual Conference on Literature and Film sponsored by the Comparative Literature Circle of the Florida State University. The nearly 200 papers read on the conference topic, *Ambiguities in Literature and Film,* represented a wide spectrum of subject matters and methods of literature and film criticism. The financial constraints of academic publishing limit our selection, and we regret that we are not able to share more of the challenging contributions to the conference with a larger audience. However, the studies included here give an indication of the range of the conference papers and of the interdisciplinary possibilities realized by the conference in exploring the common topic. The collection furthermore offers a balance of literature and film studies, as well as comparisons of literary and cinematic works. This is by coincidence, not by design, but it reflects the comparable emphases placed on the two disciplines in the conference.

We express our indebtedness to Augustus B. Turnbull, Provost of the Florida State University, for his continuing support of our conferences, and Werner A. Baum, Dean of the College of Arts and Sciences, the Florida State University, for helping to make this volume possible. We are also grateful to the Departments of Classics, English, and Modern Languages and Linguistics of the Florida State University for their backing of the conference and to Hope Kurtz, Todd Smith, Howard George, Scott Judy, and Kathleen Laufenberg for their editorial production work in preparing this text for publication.

—H. P. B.

1. INTRODUCTION: AMBIGUITIES IN LITERATURE AND FILM

Hans P. Braendlin

IT IS AN ENDURING characteristic of humankind to seek full understanding of life and the world in which it is placed. Invariably, it seems, the quest for understanding entails the encounter of ambiguity, what the dictionary defines as the quality or state of having two or more possible meanings, or being indefinite, unclear, or vague. The word *ambiguous* goes back to the Latin *ambigere* (to wander) which combines *ambi-* (about, around) with *agere* (to do, to act). The etymology implicates the occurrence and perception of ambiguity as an indefinite wandering, a continuous activity about or around meaning which is inconclusive to the extent that no central meaning becomes fixed in the process. Ambiguity, to use the semiotic terminology, arises from the presence of signs that provide insufficient direction on the road to meaning as an intended specific destination. The correlativity of ambiguity and meaning inherent in this definition may also be illustrated with the root of the word *meaning,* which denotes "opinion" or "intent." "Ambiguity" and "meaning" share the etymological base of intentionality, in the sense of purposeful motion and direction, except that "meaning" normally implies firm opinion; that is, a sign or group of signs fixes meaning, and is found sufficient, in such directed motion.

If ambiguity is a hindrance to complete understanding, as it may seem to be, the means of escaping ambiguity, then, is to identify the correct information leading to arrival and rest. This has long been the process, not only of science with the establishment of scientific laws, but also of other systematic approaches to understanding, witnessing concerted beliefs in the feasibility of unifying meanings and formulating universal truths. However, there have also been (since the beginnings of writing) expressions of a suspicion that no such correct information is available—that ambiguities cannot be resolved—in certain instances of understanding, especially in the spheres of human existence and interaction. This suspicion is widespread and extends to all areas of intellection in the modern era, to the point even that disciplines of knowledge today express concerted beliefs in the feasibility that simultaneities of different meanings persist in the things of cognitive concern.

These beliefs do not imply a necessity, on the one hand, of embracing indeterminacy or the absurd, though this is a consequence for some, or, on the other hand, of abandoning quests for harmonies of meaning. Rather, the modern orientation involves in the main a realization that, for the present at least, the activity of embracing meanings is one of *com*prehending ambiguities—that accordance of meanings is a measure of their discordance—in most instances of perception. This "realization" may be achieved in either of two senses of the word: as an apprehension of what presents itself as a predetermined ambiguity, or as a bringing about of ambiguity as the true nature of what presents itself as possessing unequivocal meaning.

The present-day realization of extensive ambiguities is, above all, a corollary of a pervasive assumption of irreducible dualisms or pluralisms at the core of things. In the new science, for instance, the traditional mandate of science for defining objective truths of nature has been weakened by a fundamental ambiguity which the theory of relativity and subatomic physics suggest: The nature of the observed may depend on the conditions of the observer in the processes of scientific investigation. Much of modern psychology occupies itself with what appears to be an irreversible separation of self and other, including the other as part of the self, confirming a suspicion of earlier humanity.

A similar situation informs the philosophy of human existence in the wake of existentialism and phenomenology. As Simone de Beauvoir points out in her *Ethics of Ambiguity,* the fundamental ambiguity of the human condition, which contains the individual's uniqueness as subject and dependence on collectivity as object, was eliminated or masked in past philosophy by recourse to a monism of

2

one sort or another.[1] Existentialism as de Beauvoir understands it, on the other hand, is a "philosophy of ambiguity" based on the assumption of an "irreducible ambiguity" of the individual's "insignificance" and "sovereign importance" (EA 9). The meaning of existence involves continuous action whose every moment is at once a "failure" and a "success" (EA 129).

The development of literature—film is, of course, a relative newcomer—does not unequivocally follow a parallel course from single to multiple meanings as documented conclusions about objects of perception. It is in the literature of the earlier times that we encounter many of the expressions whose contents suggest irresolutions of ambiguities. The authors were either unable or unwilling to admit integrations of meanings, perceiving instead their multiplicity and/or actualizing with the power of the imagination the potential for idiosyncratic expression, for protestation rather than attestation, or for confession rather than profession. Inversely, modern literature, and film as a modern art, contain works that like other literary works of earlier times suggest resolutions of ambiguities, deriving from the continuing power of art, though perhaps not only of art, to give free reign to intentions of unifying meanings through the imagination. Nevertheless, we observe frequent instances in twentieth-century literature and film of discontinuities and disjunctions of narrative structures and significations, hence of their possible meanings. Much like some of their literary predecessors, though now not necessarily for idiosyncratic reasons, the authors of such works are either unable or unwilling to admit a freedom of fantasy for integrations of meanings, sharing instead with much of twentieth-century humanity a sense of insistent ambiguities.

Furthermore, both early and modern authors may share with many present-day interpreters/critics of literature and of film (to the extent of the art's analogies to literature) the following, interrelated realizations: irreducible dualisms or pluralisms pertain to the processes of creating meanings; and the very nature of language, be it literary, cinematic, or critical, contains unresolvable ambiguities which compound or confound the means and the ends of the structures and significations of the communications. In addition to the possibility of ambiguities in the "contents" of literature and film, which may reflect an ethics or metaphysics of ambiguity on the part of the authors or perceivers in the creation of meanings, there is the strong possibility that the "forms" of the arts and of the responses to

3

them are grounded in an aesthetics of ambiguity. Plausible assumptions are made today about dualistic agencies in the creation of meanings, not only of literary or cinematic texts and readers or viewers—the "nature" of a text may depend on the conditions of the perceiver in the process of reading or viewing—but also of authors and their texts as they unfold, and of authors and "implied" perceivers. Furthermore, plausible assumptions are made about dualistic or pluralistic efficiencies of, for example, signifiers and signifieds, meanings of texts as verbal or cinematic constructs and meanings from possible correspondences of textual meanings with contexts, specifically, rhetorical and referential modes of texts in the production of meanings, or interdependencies of texts, both artistic and nonartistic, which signal possibly vast "intertextual" meanings for both authors and perceivers in correspondingly extended frameworks of references. Since such conditions are for the most part superimposable on each other, the authors and readers/viewers who share these assumptions find it difficult to escape the impression that the constituents of literature and film, indeed of language in general, consist of permanent differences rather than identities.

Above all, the realization prevails in twentieth-century criticism that ambiguity is innate to the primary mode of language, the rhetorical, and that therefore already the rhetorical aspects of cinematic as well as literary language place texts beyond conclusive intelligibility. Paul de Man suggests in the case of understanding writings (his observations are true also for film) that the referentiality of texts is, in the face of this predicament, either deferred indefinitely or assumed by a "preordained agreement . . .; this agreement however is merely contractual, never constitutive [and] every piece of writing can be questioned as to its rhetorical mode. . . ."[2] Although de Man is speaking here mainly about the continuity of all writings, his comments apply also to each moment of text-reader confrontations, including artists as readers of texts. Contractual agreements and their dissolutions involve each individual perception in its uniqueness as well as the dependence of each perception on collectivity, superimposing an ethics of ambiguity on an aesthetics of ambiguity in the interactions of authors, texts, and the interpretation of texts. This condition permits, as a complement to the invalidation of a constitutive establishment of universal meanings of texts, the invalidation of a constitutive establishment of criticism. The condition also allows for an immediacy of reviewing documented history and, if there is a contractual agreement on the reciprocity of art and life, of social change.

Although there are subtle but clear differences between literature and film, they are kindred arts. Accordingly, terms such as "text," "narrative," "rhetorical," "referential," "reading," and others, as well as many specific terms of semiotics, have been incorporated, with appropriate differentiations, into the language of film discussion. Their joint use for the two arts possesses at least a heuristic value for comparative study. The prominent difference between them consists of the superior power of cinema to create the appearance of reality and the related power of cinematic rhetoric to employ visual and audial (musical) signs in addition to verbal signs. Film adds sensory immediacy to the conveyance and perception of meanings, which may require subsequent mediation for understanding, and certainly does so for interpreting film. This places a greater emphasis than does literature on audience participation in the creation of meaning. As Robert Scholes points out, literature is at pains "to achieve some impression of the real," using "some notion of realism or verisimilitude as an evaluative standard," whereas film, by contrast, "must achieve some level of reflection, or conceptualization, in order to reach its optimum condition as narrative."[3] The special capacity for verisimilitude and sensory immediacy also allows cinema to charge its narrative with greater emotional content than literature can. Since emotion provides meanings of its own, which may require even more reflection by the audience, film provides an additional source of ambiguity. When this potential is actualized, film becomes especially difficult to understand as to its referentiality. In any case, literature and film have the common property that their meanings are never fixed and must be constantly won, in a continuous activity of understanding which is in every instance of coherent interpretation both right and wrong.

We begin the collection with an essay that argues an inevitable ambiguity of the interaction between life's realities and the imagination. Robert Kugelmann's point of view is that of a psychologist, but he gives it a broader cultural setting, including, in particular, the poetry of Wallace Stevens in his perspective. The imaginative power of poetry illuminates the primary phenomenon in the craft of psychology, which is the reciprocity of fiction and non-fiction, of escape from and return to the pressures of everyday life. The fundamental force behind the process is human stupidity, poetically well embodied in Stevens's Crispin: The inertia of stupidity dissipates the energy of imagination, grounding us again in reality, but stupidity is also the ground on which we realize the root images of life and from which imagination springs.

The two subsequent studies reveal the power of the artistic imagination to suggest a resolution of ambiguity for the authorial persona. Furthermore, the studies illustrate what may be a major tendency of artists, who use the imagination for such integration, to do so for nostalgic reasons. However, the works investigated differ greatly as to their individual intentions, which are variously metaphysical, ethical, and aesthetic in nature, and to the modes of expression as well as the artists' realization of rhetorical potentials. Dennis P. Slattery identifies Dostoevsky's "The Peasant Marey" as an extended metaphor that aids the author's memory of freedom, emancipation, and the possibility of resurrection, thus allowing the author to convert his current view of a base humanity. Dostoevsky reveals that memory is transformative, and "to say that memory is metaphorical is to implicate the memorial quality of metaphor." Deborah Glassman explains the structural relationship of Marguerite Duras's "Indian Cycle" (three novels followed by three films) by showing that fantasy functions as model for approaching the relationship between different semiotic systems of representation in the works. Fantasy "stages" a desire for a return to the past and suggests, as an accomplishment of such a return, a trajectory between the first novel, *The Ravishing of Lol V. Stein,* and the next to last film, *India Song,* two endpoints in a "formal arch between literature and film."

With the succeeding essay by Lewis A. Lawson, attention shifts to the creative power for unifying the narrated self. For Binx Bolling, the protagonist of Percy Walker's novel, *The Moviegoer,* the experience of movie-watching leads to conceptions of time and space as higher reality, which cinematography provides, but they inevitably yield again to a realization of the drab "everydayness" in ordinary time and space. The means of Binx's escape from the dilemma is love as a reflection of divine love. Ironically the resolution is implicitly prefigured in the last film that Binx will ever see, *The Young Philadelphians* ("the young inhabitants of love").

The remaining essays contain a spectrum of interpretations that apprehend ambiguities of narrative and semiotic strategies as reflections of persevering ambiguities of the authors' or protagonists' orientations and of reader responses, or that bring to the fore ambiguities which offer alternative comprehensions of the works. The first three of these essays raise questions of genre—a fundamental aspect of rhetorical criticism—in film, where such questions are particularly challenging due to the art's potential of a great richness of narrative structures and semiotic codes.

As Paul Petlewski argues, Alfred Hitchcock's *Psycho* presents an "assault on the viewer" but also a "tease" because the film alternates between the genres of realism (in the mode of the semi-documentary crime story), Gothic horror cinema, and classical detective story. Designed to mislead the audience, *Psycho* is a "chameleon film" that tests the boundaries of genre in film.

The next two papers address special uses by filmmakers of cinematic rhetoric that spell generic characteristics of their craft in general. T. J. Ross shows that Robert Aldrich's films contain ambiguities arising from an interplay between older avant-garde conventions and marginal commentaries on such conventions which subvert plot formulas and stock images. This interplay lends both a historical value and a continuing appeal to the films.

Brigitte Peucker makes the point that Rainer Werner Fassbinder's narrative strategies hinge on an interplay between melodrama ("low art") and Brechtian distanciation ("high art") as a function of an ambiguous relationship between "emotion" and "reason." The tension exists at various levels of narrative and produces meanings which are pertinent to the question of genre. In its ambiguity, the juxtaposition of emotion and reason forms an open-ended dialectic in the structures of Fassbinder's films.

The next three essays concern unresolvable ambiguities for protagonists of literary and cinematic works which implicitly or explicitly inform also authorial and interpretive points of view. F. Nick Clary's essay addresses a crucial interpretive problem of the Shakespeare canon, the character of Prince Hal. Concentrating on the protagonist's ironic language and contradictory behavior, Clary argues the consistency of Hal's ambiguous role. The nature of the pervasive ambiguity is such that the interpretation of Hal—is he Machiavellian or does he believe in redemption?—depends on the reader's assumptions about human nature and experience.

Leona Toker identifies ambiguity as the structural principle which fuses content and form in Vladimir Nabokov's *Invitation to a Beheading*. The ambiguities in the work can be resolved by a fig-

7

urative signification of the stages that mark the development of the protagonist, Cincinnatus, and of the reader's response. On the literal level, the total effect of the ambiguities is that of a dreamlike quality of the fictional world. The absence of an authority of such a reading is the recurrent basis of ambiguity. Sharing with the protagonist the belief in a "gnostic dualism" of the material and a mysterious world, Nabokov refuses to define the world of *Invitation* either realistically or supernaturally.

Robert T. Self sees in Robert Altman's *Buffalo Bill and the Indians* a "postmodern" problematics of unified character identity, textual meaning, and audience response. The compounded difficulty of the film lies in the circumstance that the textual self, the text, and the audience are products of competing authors. Possible solutions to the problem are located on a spectrum of interpretation between a symbolic reconstruction of meaning and an acceptance of the plural text with all its uncertainties.

The last two essays of the collection disclose structural and semiotic ambiguities of texts that suggest interpretations at variance with ostensible authorial intentions and/or other critical views of the works. Robert T. Eberwein confronts the critical question whether Federico Fellini's *City of Women* is male chauvinist or feminist. The charge of anti-feminism seems to be supported by the fact that Fellini makes women out of and into images, makes montages of unreal women, and thus fails to identify Woman. For a counter-argument, Eberwein relies on the critical theory of a parallel between dream and cinema. In the dream sequence, an important part of Fellini's film, the protagonist Snaporaz indeed dreams a montage of women but awakens to a new understanding of woman. Fellini, the maker of the film, could be said to share the discovery to the extent that we identify him with Snaporaz.

Mary Jane Schenck demonstrates that Flannery O'Connor's didactic-religious interpretation of her own work, with which most critics agree, is wrong or at best only partly right. O'Connor texts contain irony of the sort which Schenck, following Baudelaire and de Man, defines as a consciousness with a capacity to be both self and other; the disjunction occurs by means of language and by a transfer of the empirical self to a world constituted out of, and in, language. Two of O'Connor's short stories serve as examples of this kind of ironic language, which leads to disintegration of the self when the characters realize that the linguistic self has no grounding.

8

NOTES

[1] Simone de Beauvoir, *The Ethics of Ambiguity,* trans. Bernard Frechtman (Secaucus, N.J.: The Citadel Press, 1975) 7–8. Hereafter cited in the text as EA.

[2] Paul de Man, *Allegories of Reading: Figural Language in Rousseau, Nietzsche, Rilke, and Proust* (New Haven: Yale University Press, 1979) 204. See Jonathan Culler, *On Deconstruction: Theory and Criticism after Structuralism* (Ithaca: Cornell University Press, 1982) 251. For a discussion of modern criticism culminating in deconstruction, see also Vincent B. Leitch, *Deconstructive Criticism: An Advanced Introduction* (New York: Columbia University Press, 1983). For a statement in earlier twentieth-century criticism on unresolvable ambiguities of the rhetorical aspects of language, see Northrop Frye, *Anatomy of Criticism: Four Essays* (Princeton: Princeton University Press, 1957, repr. New York: Atheneum, 1967) 335.

[3] Robert Scholes, "Narration and Narrativity in Film," *Quarterly Review of Film Studies* 1, 3 (August 1976): 295–96. See Peter Ruppert, "Introduction: Recent Ideas of Narrative Order," in *Ideas of Order in Literature and Film: Selected Papers from the 4th Annual Florida State University Conference on Literature and Film,* ed. Peter Ruppert (Tallahassee: University Presses of Florida, 1981) 5.

2. STUPIDITY AS THE GROUND OF THE IMAGINATION: FICTION AND NONFICTION IN THE PROCESSES OF PSYCHOLOGY

Robert Kugelmann

THE POET AND POETRY are vital to the craft of psychology. I say this because poets provide the most penetrating descriptions of the world and of the soul. If poets only gave us data, they would be disposable. Poetry is essential to the health of the psychological craft because of its insistence on the imagination. Wallace Stevens writes, "Poetic value is an intrinsic value. It is not the value of knowledge. It is not the value of faith. It is the value of the imagination."[1] One virtue of the imagination is that it allows us to escape from the pressures of reality. In the escape, imagination places us in a clearing where we view ourselves and life and imagine these things anew. The depth-psychological tradition also values the imagination, seeing it as the *sine qua non* of psychological life, seeing it as another name for the psyche. However, the craft of psychology forces us to submit to the pressures of reality. Psychology has the value of the imagination, but it also has the values of knowledge and of faith. A child of philosophy and medicine, psychology embodies the ideals of understanding the world and caring for people in times of distress. The pull of these latter values has the effect of displacing the imagination. Perhaps, if we were disembodied spirits, we could attend to everything at once. Since we are not, we find ourselves immersed in the day-to-day workings of the craft.

A story is told about inmates in a concentration camp, who on one occasion refused to betray a fellow prisoner who had committed the heinous crime of stealing potatoes. For this atrocity, the camp officials denied the prisoners their already meager rations. Morale was low. The senior block warden asked one prisoner, the young psychiatrist Viktor Frankl, to say a few words of encouragement. The cold, starving, emaciated man, mustering his strength, stood before his comrades. Without denying the grim realities of concentration camp life, he tried to give them hope. And he quoted a poet: "What you have experienced, no power on earth can take away from you."[2]

This story presents the relationship of the psychologist to the work. Frankl, as observer and recorder of the story, is entangled in it. Reading his autobiographical account of his time in the concentration camp, one cannot sustain the Cartesian ideal of the detached observer, an observer who never dirties the data with traces of mortality. The psychologist belongs to and participates in the events being witnessed. Such participation needs to be more than intellectual; it must involve the person of the psychologist. Frankl was not only a comrade to these despairing men, but he faced his own despair. One senses that he met it again on the occasion described. In psychological work, the boundaries between the observer and the observed shift and blur because the subject of study matters personally to the psychologist and resonates throughout his being.

A psychologist needs, therefore, to renounce the self-image of "The sovereign ghost. As such the Socrates / Of snails, musician of pears, principium / And lex," to quote from Stevens's poem "The Comedian as the Letter C."[3] This is the psychologist's lot: anchored by flesh, bones, and culture in situations, committed to making sense of the mess, and trying to enable healing to happen. With no omniscient access to life—we have only perspectives, narrow and wide—we huddle together in universities, churches, and organizations hoping to transcend our limits.

Even our communities come to be shared points of view on the world. Following Jung, let us call these perspectives archetypes, which become our basic modes of being-in-the-world. These archetypes are the images through which we experience life, the images that form our action. Psychology, as the study of archetypes, ought

11

to give us two things: a sense of the event under discussion, such as child development, and the archetypal image that reveals the event. In other words, psychological work includes a reflective component, one that simultaneously illuminates the perspective that reveals the world, as well as the world that is revealed.

Precisely here, the ambiguity of fiction and nonfiction arises in psychology. In "Imagination as Value," Stevens writes that

> in life what is important is the truth as it is, while in arts and letters what is important is the truth as we see it. There is a real difference here even though people turn to the imagination without knowing it in life and to reality without knowing it in arts and letters.[4]

Both reality, "the truth as it is," *and* imagination, "the truth as we see it," are important for psychology. In practice there is no clear differentiation between things as they are and things as we see them. The ambiguity of fiction and nonfiction happens in our lives and is not an artifact of psychology. Imagination permeates life to such an extent that we can say that each life is a fiction, a story whose end is yet partially unwritten and whose beginning changes, depending upon the end. In the art of living we enact images or myths, and they constitute our realities. Imagination is our rock, our reality, and images rule our lives, having names like Wealth, Power, Love, and Fame.

Psychology is modern mythology, as the archetypal psychologist James Hillman states.[5] Consequently, the ambiguity of fiction and nonfiction is a primary phenomenon in our craft. So let us work within the ambiguity and see how it leads to a key issue for our craft—an issue sadly, but understandably, neglected.

Thomas Kuhn, the philosopher of science, has written about the dialectic of normal and revolutionary science; this dialectic manifests, in scientific activity, a process that occurs in all our lives. Normal science happens whenever "the individual scientist can take the paradigm for granted, and whenever he need no longer, in his major works, attempt to build his field anew, starting from first principles."[6] Normal science and the normal run-of-the-mill affairs of daily life happen when we attend to the "what" of an experience and to the world as revealed by the archetypal images we inhabit.

Analogous to an archetype is a paradigm, which Kuhn defines as

> the entire constellation of beliefs, values, techniques, and so on shared by the members of a given community. On the other hand, it denotes one sort of element in that constellation, the concrete puzzle-solutions which, employed as models or examples, can replace explicit rules as a basis for the solution of the remaining puzzles of normal science.[7]

In the second sense, a condensation of the first, a paradigm is the specific phenomenon or formula which other events resemble. The paradigm is the image in which the work of normal science finds its significance. For example, when the patient in psychoanalysis recognizes that his or her guilt is like the guilt of Oedipus, then the analytic paradigm is being inhabited. The patient, together with the analyst, is engaging in "normal" psychoanalysis. Both see the guilt as clearly *Oedipal,* but do not see it *as* Oedipal. In this normal situation, one experiences the guilt-as-Oedipal as one's reality, not as a particular way of imagining the guilt. Ordinarily, we take experience literally, on its face value, as nonfiction. William James's comment on this proclivity of consciousness is worth quoting: "As a rule we believe as much as we can. We would believe everything if we only could."[8]

Revolutionary science happens when a paradigm breaks down and when it is being replaced by another. In everyday living, the analogous event occurs when the metaphorical character of an image shows through like the bare threads of an old coat and is no longer being taken for granted. One sees that one has been experiencing through a particular image. For example, one recognizes that one has assumed that others are more valuable than oneself. A revolutionary phase entails a breakdown of an accepted reality; the world is topsy-turvy, disorienting, crazy. The focus is on imagination in its capacity to form action, thought, feeling, and perception. Psychological revolutions follow this principle, as Stevens describes it:

> The next step would be to assert that a particular image was the chief image. This is normal life, reality-focused. Again, it would be the merest improvisation to say of any image of the world, even

though it was an image with which a vast accumulation of imaginations had been content, that it was the chief imagination. The imagination itself would not remain content with it nor allow us to do so. It is the irrepressible revolutionist.[9]

Calling the imagination a revolutionist is most apt since the appearance of imagination turns life around—or at least threatens to. Confronting an image, the words of the poet Rilke touch us: "You must change your life."[10]

Normally, that is, most of the time, we are insensitive to the images we enact; we are simply in them, occupied with the cares and pleasures of reality, as reality presents itself contoured by our "native" images. We do things unreflectively, out of habit. We are all Crispins (the hero of "The Comedian as the Letter C") in this regard: "the quotidian saps philosophers / And men like Crispin like them in intent, / If not in will, to track the knaves of thought" (72). Daily routine drains Crispin of the imagination. "Will" here refers to the imagination as Stevens spoke of it: "a principle of the mind's being, striving to realize itself in knowing itself."[11] The humdrum of life saps us of this principle, and we participate passively in our images.

Imagination, in short, requires effort, and energy is a scarce resource in anyone. The pull of practicality usually gets credit for our settling back down to normal life again. Revolutions are transitory as well as disruptive. Awareness of the imaginal character of life stops us from living straightforwardly and "naively" within the image. But life marches on, and our cares wear us down. Practicalities aside, including those in psychology arising from our values of knowledge and faith, another and less flattering element returns us to the quotidian: *stupidity*. Human stupidity as a dampening of the reverberations of the imagination grounds us again in the humdrum rut of life. I do not intend this as a critique of stupidity. On the contrary, in attenuating our sensitivity to the imaginal character of life, stupidity serves the vital role of making real the root images of life.

"Nota: stupidity is the ground of imagination." Moments, centuries of being stupid provide the sediment, the gum and goo, from which springs the life of imagination, which Stevens calls "the only true genius."[12] By stupidity I do not mean a lack of intelligence or insight or, indeed, an absence of anything whatsoever. Stupidity

14

is an active force or power in human affairs, which makes nonfiction of our fictions, reality of our imaginings. Stupidity marks the inertia constituent of human nature, the density, the solidity, the sluggishness of our being. Wallace Stevens's Crispin personifies our stupidity. This inert poet—the poem reads as his obituary—is no aberration of the imagination. Crispin embodies the stupidity which plunges us into the literalisms of life, the return from the place of imagining; stupidity is a necessary ingredient of imagination. This return makes possible future stirrings of imagination. In much the same way, the dampening of a note on a guitar string enables and makes necessary a new and unconceived song.

To understand the role of stupidity, let us consider briefly the happening of imagination. Imagination announces itself in the phenomenon of reverberation. Reverberation signifies here the stirring of a transformation in existence, a change initiated and formed by the image one reads or hears, taking the poetic image as paradigm. Ricoeur describes the reverberations of an image as a radiation of the image and its significance "in all directions, reanimating earlier experiences, awakening dormant memories, spreading to adjacent sensorial fields."[13] Bachelard expresses this with greater eloquence:

> The resonances are dispersed on the different planes
> of our life in the world, while the repercussions in-
> vite us to give greater depth to our own existence. In
> the resonance we hear the poem, in the reverber-
> ations we speak it, it is our own. The reverberations
> bring about a change of being.[14]

The image vitalizes life. When the image resounds, one remains under the spell of the poem and inhabits a fictional space.

Since we always dwell in some image, we can say that the reverberations of that image are present everywhere and always. They are present as lines of force or vectors which map out the paths we follow. The articulations of our native images are, however, solidified, the reverberations turned rut. The images have lost the vitality of the imagination, at least in an active sense. The imagining happens, in the normal state of affairs, unconsciously, unreflectively. Our inability to perceive its occurrence and to be in tune with its resonances defines our stupidity. I take stupidity in its primary sense of dullness, density of mentality. Experiences of stupidity accentuate our bondedness to the earth. Some of the usages of the word make this clear. In the word's history, such things as stones, animals, matter, emotions, and so forth have been singled out as stupid in an exemplary manner. The following homely sentiment expressed by Dryden is typical, "But I esteem the Faith of a stupid Peasant, more than all the Lessons of Socrates."[15] The more inert, dense, material, and earth-bound something or someone is or appears to be, the more stupid that thing or that person is said to be.

By bringing stupidity, with its root sense of "being stunned" or "benumbed," into conjunction with the idea of the reverberations of the imagination, we shift from a view of stupidity simply as an absence of "intelligence" to one that emphasizes the earthiness of human being. We are mediums that can receive the resonances of imagination, which give us depth, but, as mediums, we offer resistance to them. The quicksilver of fantasy drains from us, and we stand around scratching our heads, those lumps of gray and white matter.

When we view stupidity in its connection with imagination, we begin to see the role of the former in grounding the latter. In our stupidity, we take the fictions of the imagination as realities, as we conform to the stirrings of fantasy. To be stupid means, in other words, to be literal-minded. We lose the play of meaning of an image as it settles down and becomes a univocal truth. What is fictional, in a moment of imagining, now becomes "real" as the reverberations harden within the thickness of our skulls. Its literal-mindedness gives stupidity a decidedly comic appearance: the human as clown, buffoon, or Simple Simon. Phenomenological philosophy calls this dampening of an image the process of sedimentation, which names the calcification of insight and metaphor into habit. The habitual world, especially as it shapes expectations, is the "real world": reality is what we unreflectively expect to happen. Stupidity serves as valet here, stiffening our resistance to insight and image.

Sedimented images are "reality." Using language that partakes in the reverberation metaphor, William James characterizes our sense of reality as

> the cessation of theoretic agitation, through the advent of an idea which is inwardly stable, and which fills the mind solidly to the exclusion of contradictory ideas. When this is the case, motor effects are apt to

follow. Hence the states of consent and belief, characterized by repose on the intellectual side, are both
intimately connected with subsequent practical
activity.[16]

We sense reality, James continues, in whatever hits home: the body,
the self, the tangible, the familiar, or, in general terms, whatever
matters or has an effect. In line with this depiction of our sense of
reality, James quotes Josiah Royce to the effect that human thought
follows the "law of least effort."[17] This tendency to least effort, or
homeostasis as it is now called, names the phenomenon of stupidity
from a kinder direction. All these ideas including sedimentation, the
"cessation of theoretic agitation," and the "law of least effort"
indicate that inertia of human existence which, while making us
immune to the workings of imagination, ground us and bring us
home again.[18]

The movement of "The Comedian as the Letter C" is precisely
a movement to home. The story line follows Crispin as emigrant to
America, and plots his plodding poetics and the establishment of his
home and family. The story gives us an image of the stupidity which
fosters future imagining; the poem's ambiguous conclusion forces
the reader to imagine beyond both Crispin and the poem's point of
view. One only uneasily identifies, or feels at home, with either, and
this keeps us imagining and not formulating doctrine "from the rout"
(74).

Whenever Crispin meets with agitation, the echoings or rum-
blings of some image, he reaches to imagine. First the sea dissolves
him:

> [He] now beheld himself,
> A skinny sailor peering in the sea-glass.
> What word split up in clickering syllables
> And storming under multitudinous tones
> Was name for this short-shanks in all that brunt?
> Crispin was washed away by magnitude. (58–59)

The sea as noise, the reverberations of demythologizing, over-
whelms Crispin and destroys his former reality of "simple salad
beds" (58). In the Yucatan, the violent fecundity of the jungle sparks
his revised poetics. The narrator presents this with acidity:

17

> He was in this as other freemen are,
> Sonorous nutshells rattling inwardly.
> His violence was for aggrandizement
> And not for stupor, such as music makes
> For sleepers halfway waking. (61)

The flush of Crispin's poetic passion is, in other words, a stupor. The reverberations of the tropics and the rattling lull him to sleep, even as he believes he has uncovered the truth. Yet the acid of the narrator's irony fails to convince us completely, for Crispin's imaginative insights have validity. In short, we can neither accept without reserve Crispin's "Green barbarism turned paradigm" (61) nor identify with the narrator. This is unsettling and we wonder: Are our imaginings any different from the hollow rattling of a nutshell? Do we pass from imaging to stupor as the reverberations of images lull us to sleep in their attenuation?

In part, Crispin's stupidity is one with his egotism. His aggrandizement is self-aggrandizement. Even in his fatalist demise, he remains the insatiable egotist:

> Should he lay by the personal and make
> Of his own fate an instance of all fate?
> What is one man among so many men?
> What are so many men in such a world?
> Can one man think one thing and be it long?
> . . . .
> For realist, what is is what should be. (71)

His egotism, as this passage shows, makes of the ego a grand center of the universe even in the very thought of one's own meaninglessness. Stupidity entails a narrowing of one's perspective, a narrowing *to* one perspective, a sedimentation in one mode of being. In our stupidity, the world—things as they are—is what we see of it. This accounts for the arrogance of stupidity and the intransigence of the ego.[19] Crispin plans, midway through the poem, a new poetics inspired by the idea of the imagination as grounded in the soil: "Nota: his soil is man's intelligence" (66). Such a position has its merits in Stevens's poetics. In a later poem entitled "A Mythology Reflects Its Region," Stevens writes,

> The image must be of the nature of its creator.
> It is the nature of its creator increased,
> Heightened. It is he, anew, in a freshened youth
> And it is he in the substance of his region,
> Wood of his forest and stone out of his fields
> Or from under his mountain. (398)

Imagination is the stirring of the earth, the human soil, dirt, and mess of our lives and times. How gossip rouses fantasies and more! Crispin recognizes that imagination means the giving to voice the regions of the world; that imagination makes the earth sing or is the resonance of the earth. But he literalizes his project:

> Upon these premises propounding, he
> Projected a colony. . . .
> The man in Georgia walking among pines
> Should be pines-spokesman.The responsive man,
> Planting his pristine cones in Florida,
> Should prick thereof, not on the psaltery,
> But on the banjo's categorical gut,
> Tuck, tuck, while the flamingos flapped his bays.
> (68)

Crispin's way of being in the image inevitably leads to nowhere except a "Nice Shady Home." Crispin rings with the image as though he were a lump of lead. He is the soil of man's imagination.[20] In the final two sections of the poem, Stevens most clearly presents the image of stupidity as the earth of imagination. As Crispin stays put in America, his wonderful plans fade.

He slowly settles down until he literally or figuratively rests in uneasy peace in that ground. The loss of imagination as an active force happens:

> But day by day, now this thing and now that
> Confined him, while it cosseted, condoned,
> Little by little, as if the suzerain soil
> Abashed him by carouse to humble yet
> Attach. (70)

Nothing in this homey place, and we must see these sections as describing "home" for us all, reverberates. "The words of things entangle and confuse. / The plum survives its poems. . . it survives in its own form" (70). His world is narrowed to "Shall or ought to be in is " (70), and to his cabin. He no longer doubts, no longer questions, no longer stirs his world. It is reality—what is, things as they are. He fathers daughters, not poems; his children, "True daughters both of Crispin and his clay" (73), are called "Four questioners and four sure answerers" (74).

Crispin as Candide, with the attending lack of theoretic agitation and the sedimentation of his existence, marks the imprint of stupidity. Crispin in his rut, in his frozen metaphor, embodies the dullness and numbness of stupidity. By reading the final image of earth as a metonymy, we can see that Crispin, the poet, is

> . . . . a turnip, once so readily plucked,
> Sacked up and carried overseas, daubed out
> Of its ancient purple, pruned to the fertile main,
> And sown again by the stiffest realist,
> Came reproduced in purple, family font,
> The same insoluble lump. (74)

Crispin is the turnip of the imagination, the lump from which its ancient purple arises.

Crispin is, in this way, everyman. The poem is a fanfare for the common man, or a fanfare for the inertia which makes us all common. But this music does stick, as the narrator suggests. Crispin is "a profitless / Philosopher, beginning with green brag, / Concluding fadedly . . . proving what he proves / Is nothing" (75).

Crispin personifies the failures of the imagination. He is the stupidity of life, that inertial force in us that renders us insensitive to the images that shape life. Crispin is doomed from the beginning, since throughout his journey he sought, not the images per se as a value, but the doctrine he could concoct, the images that with his quill he could catechize. Not content with the fictional space of reverberating images, he desired continuously the solid unmoving ground of reality. Crispin illustrates that stupidity is a desire for earth, for body, for place, for a unity with ground. Far from being a consequence of the passivity of matter, or of a lack of wit, stupidity is a desire to affirm kinship with the earth and its inertia. Stupidity declares our identity with earth.

20

In *The Necessary Angel,* Stevens writes that imagination extends to everything the peculiarity of nobility. He begs off defining nobility because "if it is defined, it will be fixed and it must not be fixed."[21] It must not be fixed because it concerns the reverberations of things throughout the depths and heights of the psyche. And he says of the nobility of the imagination: "It is a violence from within that protects us from the pressure of reality."[22] The imagination ennobles by making things glow, radiate, resonate. Yet it needs its valet, gentle Crispin, that clown of the imagination, who helps us trip into reality. We stumble into nonfiction both in life and in psychological work. Stupidity, token of our feet and heads of clay, shows us as lumps, insoluble, that the imagination can, at times, make noble.

NOTES

[1] Wallace Stevens, *The Necessary Angel: Essays on Reality and the Imagination* (New York: Vintage Books, 1951) 149.

[2] Viktor Frankl, *Man's Search for Meaning* (New York: Washington Square Press, 1963) 131.

[3] *The Palm at the End of the Mind,* ed. Holly Stevens (New York: Vintage Books, 1971) 58. Unless otherwise stated, the poetry of Wallace Stevens is quoted from this edition, with the permission of the publisher.

[4] *The Necessary Angel,* 147.

[5] James Hillman, *Re-Visioning Psychology* (New York: Harper and Row, 1975) 154.

[6] Thomas Kuhn, *The Structure of Scientific Revolutions* (Chicago: University of Chicago Press, 1970) 19–20.

[7] Kuhn, 175.

[8] William James, *The Principles of Psychology* (1890; reprinted, New York: Dover, 1950) 2:299.

[9] *The Necessary Angel,* 151–52.

[10] Rainer Maria Rilke, *Selected Poems of Rainer Maria Rilke,* trans. Robert Bly (New York: Harper and Row, 1981) 147.

[11] *The Necessary Angel,* 10.

[12] J. Hillis Miller, *Poets of Reality* (Cambridge: Belknap Press of Harvard University Press, 1965) 258.

[13] Paul Ricoeur, "Imagination in Discourse and in Action," in *Analecta Husserliana,* ed. A. Tymieniecka (Dordrecht, Holland: D. Reidel, 1978) 7:8.

[14] Gaston Bachelard, *The Poetics of Space,* trans. Maria Jolas (Boston: Beacon Press, 1964) xviii.

[15] *Saint-Euremond's Miscellaneous Essays,* quoted in *The Oxford English Dictionary,* 9th Printing.

[16] *Principles of Psychology*, 2:283–84.

[17] *The Religious Aspect of Philosophy,* quoted in *Principles of Psychology,* 2:316.

[18] To be more complete, Freud's understanding of the conservative character of the instincts could be added. Their inertia renders us archaic even when civilized.

[19] Jung "defines" stupidity as the belief that "man *is* merely what his consciousness knows of itself." C.G. Jung, *The Undiscovered Self,* trans. R. F. C. Hull (New York: Mentor Books, 1958) 107–08.

[20] For more on the connection between earth and poetic inspiration, see the penetrating essay of David Lavery, "'The Genius of the Sea': Wallace Stevens' 'The Idea of Order at Key West,' Stanislaw Lem's *Solidaris,* and the Earth as a Muse," *Extrapolation* 21, 2:101–05.

[21] *The Necessary Angel*, 36.

[22] *The Necessary Angel*, 36.

3. IS MEMORY METAPHORICAL OR IS METAPHOR MEMORIAL? DOSTOEVSKY'S "THE PEASANT MAREY"

Dennis P. Slattery

THE CURRENT LITERATURE on metaphor is so thick and varied, as Wayne Booth notes, that the winds of confusion, not the calmer air of clarity, surround the forest of this figure. His prediction that we shall have by the year 2039 more "metamorticians" (embalmers of dead metaphors) than people, given the current growth rate, causes one to hesitate before becoming yet another member of such a mighty vanguard.[1] Still, might there be room for one more initiate into the rite of passage between the literal and figurative gates of language? "Metaphor is a dreamwork," writes Davidson, "and like all dreamwork, its interpretation reflects as much on the interpreter as on the originator."[2]

I wish to complicate the dreamwork for a moment, to wake it up and ask it to remember in order to see if anything can be made of the question: "Is memory metaphorical or is metaphor memorial?" While there is no universally accepted definition of metaphor, a term that—like "existentialism," or "intellectual," or even "teacher of rhetoric"—may be defined for the immmediate occasion, I would use a most general description which should offend no one: "metaphors represent the facts of one sort in an idiom appropriate to another."[3] Extending this definition, Turbayne suggests that metaphors are sort-crossings; we observe one thing in terms of another.

Is this duality of seeing a natural part of memory? Is to remember to create metaphor? Does memory have the ability to order reality by means of metaphor-making? To begin to answer some of these questions I turn to Dostoevsky's *Diary of a Writer* of February 1876. Here he relates an incident involving himself and a peasant named Marey who worked for his father. What interests me is the overlay of time in the story and how the recollection of the peasant Marey came to him at a time of intense suffering. Dostoevsky was, he recalls in 1876, a prisoner in a Siberian camp in 1850 when he remembered the story of his youth as a boy of nine. While he recollects the peasant Marey in 1850, he writes the memory down in the *Diary* some twenty-six years later, as a recollection of a recollection. The 1850 memory is ordered, detailed, and precise; the conditions out of which it grew were, on the contrary, chaotic, dangerous, painful, and dispiriting. The 1850 memory is scorpioid, circinate, folding back on itself and recaptured in 1876. Does memory then promote order within disorder; does one, especially during times of anguish and intense suffering or when one is cast into an unpropitious world, remember images which promise stability and order? If so, is metaphor part of this remembrance?

First I would consider the temporal stratification in which the memory occurs. In 1876, at the age of fifty-five, Dostoevsky writes in the *Diary* of a memory of himself in Siberia in 1850 when he is twenty-nine years old. As he writes, he remembers himself in Siberia on the second day of Easter week. The prisoners, left to themselves, unguarded, carry on in drunken and often brutal merriment. They beat one another, steal from one another, and abuse whoever crosses their path. Many convicts, near death from rather ambitious beatings, lay on the floor covered with sheepskins. Dostoevsky writes that he remembers feeling gloomy, then increasingly angry; a Polish prisoner passes him and snarls,"Je hais ces brigands!" (How I hate these brigands!)[4] Dostoevsky returns to his bunk in the barracks and, lying on his back with hands clasped behind his head, begins to meditate on his past life, recalling his years in servitude. He becomes self-forgetful and allows recollections to invade his mind "of their own accord," and, as he tells us, "only on rare occasions did I evoke them by a deliberate effort of my will. It used to begin with some speck, some trait—at times almost imperceptible—and then, gradually, it would grow into a complete picture—some strong and solid impression" (207). Dostoevsky offers us the memory of his past, but is there not something of the metaphorical in what he writes next? "I used to analyze these impressions, adding new touches to things long ago outlived, and —what is more important—I used to correct, continually correct them. Therein lay my whole diversion" (207).

I am indebted to Jackson for contributing an important essay on the creative process of Dostoevsky.[5] To Jackson's conception of the triple vision of "The Peasant Marey," I wish to add a fourth shortly. His article reveals how the act of remembering and correcting those memories constitutes the creative process of the writer. Jackson also returns to the earlier entries of the *Diary* to explore how they signal the memory of the peasant Marey, for they deal with the value of the common Russian man. My interest, however, is more limited—to understand how what one remembers relates to metaphor. I wish to take another step into the Russian writer's imaginative landscape, to understand how metaphor, if extended, leads us into the fertile–dual ground of allegory.

In 1876 Dostoevsky pleads for tolerance for the simple Russian soul, composed of both scoundrel and saint, diamond and filth: "Judge the Russian people," he writes, "not by those villainies which they frequently perpetrate but by those great and holy things for which they long amidst the very villainy" (202). Then he recalls his years in Siberia, the cruel, inhumane actions of the peasant convicts in 1850; in this setting he remembers the generosity of the peasant Marey in 1830. Taken together, both recollections begin to reflect an extended metaphor of the Russian soul's duality. The memory of himself at age nine, when he is frightened by a hallucination of someone calling "a wolf's coming" (208), becomes a metaphor of his own condition in Siberia twenty years later. To understand how this is so, we must note the connections between the two events—Siberia in 1850 and the village in the summer of 1830.

The village of 1830 in August is comfortable and secure for the youth. Dostoevsky remembers not wanting to leave for Moscow to begin his French studies which will "weary" him all winter. His present state at age twenty-nine, lying on his back in the Siberian prison barrack in order to escape the cruelty of the drunken peasants, is analogous to that sweet summer of freedom ("people will not annoy a sleeping person, and yet one may be meditating and thinking" [206]). The young boy then leaves the village and climbs to the "Losk," a thick shrubbery on the far side of a ravine he has just crossed. He plunges deeper into the bushes from where he hears "a solitary peasant plowing" and coaxing his horse on with the words, "giddap—giddap!" (207). The boy does not recognize the peasant Marey, who works for his father; he was too busy "trying to break a walnut whip for myself, to hit frogs" (207)—an activity he enjoys when not engaged in his favorite hobby, Dostoevsky remembers, of collecting insects and beetles. Just prior to his remembrance in 1850 Dostoevsky was surrounded by men being beaten; a Tartar by the name of Gazin had been especially abused. The image of insects is an appropriate one for his vision of the Russian convicts who, he writes, behave like vermin and are "hideous and nasty" (207).

Suddenly the boy of nine hears in his mind the cry, "a wolf's coming," a threat which sends him running from the thicket toward the peasant who is plowing. The wolf would appear to be functioning here metaphorically as an image of fear itself, in that shortly before remembering this incident in 1850, Dostoevsky had bolted out of his barracks "like a madman" to escape the sight of six peasants beating into unconsciousness the Tartar Gazin, as the boy of nine planned to beat the frogs with his walnut switch. Metaphor and memory converge in his experience of terror and panic. The memory is metaphorical. But has it been tampered with, or, to use Dostoevsky's own word, "corrected"? I do not believe one can say for certain. We do notice the similarity between the terrified boy of nine rushing out of the shrubbery toward the solitary peasant whom he does not know and the terrified Siberian prisoner running from his barracks to escape the cruelty of the drunken peasants. But to whom or what does he run? To the memory of the peasant Marey.

The peasant interrupts his plowing to comfort the frightened youth, saying to him, "Do stop fearing. Christ be with thee. Cross thyself" (208). When the young boy does not respond, the peasant, Dostoevsky recalls, reached out to sooth his terror:

> Slowly he stretched out his thick finger, with
> the black nail soiled with earth, and gently,
> touched my trembling lips. "See! Oh!" and he
> looked at me with a long motherly smile.
> "Well, Christ be with thee. Now go." (209)

The peasant asks that the boy remember Christ. The sign of

the cross is an emblem of remembrance; remember the flogged and beaten Christ who suffered so that men might be emancipated from sin. This action is the fourth remembrance. Its intention is to dispel the hallucination of the voice crying wolf. The young Dostoevky quiets down after crossing himself, and sure that the peasant is protecting him with his gaze, walks toward home, looking back every ten steps to see if the peasant was still watching him, protecting him with his vision. The boy's glance backward as he heads securely toward home without fear offers yet another level of remembrance. The literal action of glancing back becomes a figurative act of memory.

Writing of this experience in 1876, Dostoevsky remarks how clear and precise was this remembrance originally in 1850 while lying on his bunk. So powerful was the memory, he recalls, that when he sat up in bed he continued recollecting for several more minutes. The image of the smiling, loving peasant who helped him in his fright returns as the dominant figure (Jackson rightly calls the peasant an icon) in his experience.

Now, in the frozen, brutal world of Siberia, Dostoevsky envisions all the convicts with new eyes. He sees them through the metaphor—the figure—of his experience with the peasant Marey. The convicts have been transformed by way of his remembrance in that each now has the potential to be Marey. The kind peasant is an emblem of all peasantry for the Russian prisoner: "and suddenly, by some miracle, all the hatred and anger completely vanished from my heart." And yet, the Dostoevsky of 1876 questions whether it is possible to know for certain if these convicts contain such goodness within themselves "for I have no way of peering into the human heart" (210).

Clearly the remembrance of Dostoevsky the prisoner speaks metaphorically of his present condition in 1850 in the same way that the sudden remembrance of this memory by Dostoevsky the writer in 1876 speaks metaphorically of his present interest—the goodness of the Russian peasantry—even while their manners would support the view of a people debauched and cruel. But there is another element here which is common to all of the memories: resurrection and emancipation. All of the memories contain the metaphor of new life, rebirth, new beginnings. For example, consider for a moment that Dostoevsky in 1876 pleads for a renewal of faith in Russian peasantry, for their future transformation because he believes they contain in germinal form the sacred qualites which they desire. Holiness, he believes, will one day be the dominant state of the Russian peasant which will inform all of his actions. He recalls next the Easter week in Siberia, a time when, through Christ's suffering, death, and resurrection all men may be emancipated from the shackles of sin. Redemption is a possibility for man, promised him through the resurrection. In this season he recalls the young Dostoevsky who is liberated from his fear by the peasant who will himself soon be emancipated as a serf. Marey calls on the memory of Christ to assuage the boy's panic.

Resurrection and emancipation, freedom and generosity— these actions would seem to reflect Dostoevsky's own intentional relation to his people in the present writing of 1876, earlier in 1850, and earlier still, in 1830. Writing in 1876 of Easter week in Siberia of 1850 and of August in his village in 1830, one a world of debauchery and filth, the other full of charity and holiness, allows Dostoevsky to accept the paradox of the peasant's soul composed of diamonds and filth.

Does his memory re-order events by way of metaphor, or does metaphor remember in a particular way to bring a unity, a sense of a formed experience, to what is recalled? Do we say that memory has its own life, or that metaphor remembers? One might wish to agree with Robert Frost when he asserts that metaphor constitutes the whole of thinking.[6] One would not disagree with Booth's assertion that "a metaphor cannot be judged without reference to a context "[7] which would implicate memory. I ask that you remember the story of the peasant Marey while I briefly recall the myth of memory. In the *Theogony* Hesiod tells us that Mnemosyne was the daughter of Earth (Ge) and sky (Uranos). Uranos, you remember, was the first son of Ge, who had been born out of chaos. Earth and sky mate and create memory.

Does the myth suggest to us that memory is a way out of chaos? Is it that to be without memory is to slide into chaos, to invite chaos, to be without a context? To remember is to have a place or a ground, to be earth-connected, while having the possibility for transcendence, to look skyward. Mnemosyne, we know, is also associated with springs, both in the underworld and in the upper world.[8] Springs are beginnings, origins, germs, or specks, to use Dostoevsky's language when he recounts the act of memory, out of which

28

grow whole pictures or images. The term "memory banks" may be more accurate mythically than we had formerly supposed if it is understood not as a vault but as the edge of earth which keeps the flow of memory contained so that it does not spill over its lip into forgetfulness, Lesmosyne, the daughter of Mnemosyne.

From Mnemosyne spring the nine Muses who inspire those proficient in the arts.[9] Kerényi adds that "he whom they loved, from his mouth [or pen!] poured sweet the speech and sweet the song."[10] The Muses, as inspirations to create, harbor the seeds of metaphor. If Mnemosyne's offspring are musical, may they not also be metaphorical? Dostoevsky's recollection of a recollection which, through the sign of the cross, asks once more for remembrance, might be understood as a memory expanding into a metaphor that, when extended, offers an allegory of resurrection on several levels at once; its final purpose is a shift in attitude. "An effective metaphor," states Max Black, "acts as a screen, through which we look at the world; it filters the facts, suppressing some and emphasizing others. It brings forward aspects that might not be seen at all through another medium."[11]

The medieval scholastics, fascinated by this relation of memory to metaphor, associated the act of remembering with metaphorical images. Boncompagno, writing in Bologna in 1235, defined memory as "a glorious and admirable gift of nature by which we recall past things, we embrace present things, and we contemplate future things *through their likeness to past things"* (italics mine).[12] Albertus Magnus revealed how images are an aid to memory when he suggested that "while actual facts (propria) give more exact information about the thing itself, metaphors (metaphorica) move the soul more and therefore better help the memory."[13] His work on memory and image grew out of work done earlier by Tullius who had already confirmed with what greater ease facts may be retained if translated into images.

Dostoevsky's "The Peasant Marey" is an extended metaphor whose purpose is to aid the memory, to help us remember the action of freedom, emancipation, resurrection, actions with which Dostoevsky was concerned for almost one-half century of his life. It is his controlling metaphor through which he envisions man's hope. His hope that mankind will move forward to a golden age of brotherhood, however ideal or naive we may want to judge such a vision, is nonetheless offered here in the *Diary* of 1876, with its origins forty-six years earlier in the hallucination of a frightened boy and the charity and generosity of a peasant tilling the soil with the dirt firmly entrenched under his fingernails. In an Aristotelian sense, Dostoevsky's resolution remembers the complication.

One remembers the past, but from what we have observed, the past is not recollected as fact but as image. The images are metaphorical because they reveal an interrelatedness, a likeness, among past, present, and future. Remembered images are ways of seeing; their persuasive force resides in their ability to transform attitudes and beliefs toward the present and the future.

As a result of his remembering the peasant Marey, Dostoevsky's vision of his coarse, brutal companions has been transformed —now they all contain the germ or possibility of being the peasant Marey in their hearts.

By means of metaphor Dostoevsky has glimpsed what is absent, what is not readily visible; he has indeed seen into their hearts—memory's metaphorical aspect has allowed a vision of the invisible. "A good metaphor," writes Turbayne, "sometimes enables us to learn more about the things illustrated, and through it, more about the nature of its literal meaning."[14] And later, on seeing through metaphor, he suggests one sees "the thing illustrated by means of new spectacles that, when worn for a while, are hard to discard."[15]

Dostoevsky's attitude toward the Russian folk has been incarnated in the memory of the plowing peasant and the nine-year-old youth. Visible images lead him to invisible qualities, presences, ideas, and beliefs. Dostoevsky's literal remembrance re-orders, re-forms experience, finally, in language; the literal assumes properties of metaphor. Out of the transformation arises knowledge and new attitudes. Experience now has a form. It has become part of a tradition through memory. The young boy looking back at the smiling peasant as he moves forward toward the security of home is a curative journey. The remembered presence of Marey relieves his terror; it is a reminder that his terror has been annulled. Memory, Dostoevsky reveals, is transformative: to say that memory is metaphorical is to implicate the memorial quality of metaphor.

The story "The Peasant Marey," remembered in 1850 and recollected again in 1876, invites a meditation; it asks that we think about the relation of one thing to another and to see the meaning resting between them. In the metaxis of the two, attitudes are transformed and beliefs are formed.

Chronological Scheme of Events and Events Remembered:

1876: Dostoevsky remembers his years in Siberia, especially the second day of Easter week, 1850. He records his memory of this day in *The Diary of a Writer*.

1850: Dostoevsky, in a Siberian prison camp, escapes the brutality of the convicts by meditating on his past. He recalls himself at age nine being comforted by the peasant Marey.

1830: Dostoevsky, age nine, is frightened by a hallucination of someone warning him of a wolf.

1830: The peasant Marey crosses himself and the boy and asks that Christ protect him (a remembrance of both crucifixion and resurrection).

NOTES

[1] Wayne Booth, "Metaphor as Rhetoric: The Problem of Evaluation," in *On Metaphor,* ed. Sheldon Sacks (Chicago: University of Chicago Press, 1979) 47.

[2] Donald Davidson, "What Metaphors Mean," in *On Metaphor,* ed. Sheldon Sacks (Chicago: University of Chicago Press, 1979) 29.

[3] Colin Turbayne, *The Myth of Metaphor,* rev. ed. (Columbia: University of South Carolina Press, 1971) 12.

[4] Fyodor Dostoevsky, *The Diary of a Writer,* trans. Boris Brasol (New York: George Braziller Co., 1954) 206.

[5] Robert Louis Jackson, "The Triple Vision: Dostoevsky's 'The Peasant Marey,' " *Yale Review,* Winter 1978: 225–35.

[6] Robert Frost, "Education by Poetry: A Meditative Monologue," in *The Norton Reader,* 5th abbr. ed., ed. Arthur M. Eastman (New York: W.W. Norton and Co., 1980) 250.

[7] Booth, 58.

[8] Hesiod, *Theogony,* trans. Norman O. Brown (New York: Bobbs-Merrill Co., 1953) 58.

[9] *The Meridian Handbook of Classical Mythology,* ed. Edward Tripp (New York: New American Library, 1970) 385.

[10] Károly Kerényi, *The Gods of the Greeks,* trans. Norman Cameron (London: Thames and Hudson, 1951) 103.

[11] Turbayne, 21.

[12] Frances Yates, *The Art of Memory* (Chicago: University of Chicago Press, 1966) 67.

[13] Yates, 65.

[14] Turbayne, 102.

[15] Turbayne, 103.

4. MARGUERITE DURAS'S "INDIAN CYCLE": THE FANTASY TEXT

Deborah Glassman

MARGUERITE DURAS IS a contemporary French writer who has been making films for the past twenty years. She is best known for her first collaborative effort with Alain Resnais, which produced the 1959 darling of the *Cahiers du Cinéma. Hiroshima mon amour* was Resnais's first feature-length film, and it was widely acclaimed for its cinematic treatment of the peculiar logic of memory. Duras's screenplay was less well-received. Her oftentimes disjunctive dialogue was disparaged by some as too literary. In the sixties Duras's name slipped from the public eye. But Duras's work did come to enjoy the accolades of an enthusiastic, if peripheral, group of feminists, structuralists, participants in Jacques Lacan's seminars on Freud, and critics who share an interest in semiotics and theories of the subject. In the last five years, Duras has triumphed over the critical misprision that thwarted her early work. And while her 1975 film, *India Song*, spent six years in transit between Paris and the little Carnegie where it made its official American premiere,[1] it is primarily thanks to *India Song* that Duras's work has generated significant interest and excitement for a wider audience.

India Song has been pointed to as a revolutionary film for its radical disjunction between sound track and visuals. Duras has, in fact, described it as two films, a visual track and a sound track. But *India Song* is more than just an innovative film, noteworthy for its

33

place in the history of cinema. It is the capstone work, or, rather, it is part of twin capstones for a larger network of texts which Marie-Claire Ropars aptly christened the "Indian Cycle."[2] The "Indian Cycle" is comprised of three novels and three films that appeared between 1964 and 1976. *Le Ravissement de Lol V. Stein (The Ravishing of Lol V. Stein)*, a novel published in 1964, inaugurates the "Indian Cycle." Two films, *India Song*, 1975, and *Son Nom de Vénise dans Calcutta désert (Her Venetian Name in Deserted Calcutta)*, 1976, which make economic use of a shared sound track, are the twin endpoints of the group. Duras's "Indian Cycle" moves, then, from novel to film. I would like to address the question of the structural relationship binding this group of works whose endpoints describe a wide formal arch between literature and cinema.

Most critics interested in any of the texts in the "Indian Cycle" have limited themselves to individual works and have ignored the peculiar coherence of the group as a whole. These works serve each other as pre-texts, and as sources for ulterior reworkings. Two of the novels became sources for later films; *Le Vice Consul (The Vice Consul)*, 1966, is the basis for the 1975 film, *India Song*; *L'Amour (Love)* became *La Femme du Ganges (Woman of the Ganges)* in 1972. *Le Ravissement de Lol V. Stein* was never made into a film. The film *India Song* splits its visuals and sound track which, like a strand of DNA, produces another visual film, *Son Nom de Vénise dans Calcutta désert*, a year later. In addition to this internal formal reworking of textual material, the works in the "Indian Cycle" cohere in what we can call, for the moment and for lack of a better term, a chronology. This chronology could roughly be constructed as follows. In *Le Ravissement de Lol V. Stein,* a young woman is jilted by her lover and never recovers. Lol, the eponymous heroine, returns to the scene of her jilting years later in *L'Amour*. In *India Song,* the "other woman" and Lol's fickle ex-fiancé end up in Calcutta. *Le Vice Consul*, a story written by an embassy staff member, recounts the tale of a wandering beggar woman who is shunned by her family because of an illegitimate pregnancy. She makes her way from Cambodia to Calcutta, losing her child and eventually going mad. This woman stalks the French embassy, her cries punctuate the air; she is part of the trio of heroines in these texts. *Le Ravissement de Lol V. Stein* is the prehistory for the group; *India Song* is its memory. By "prehistory" and "memory" I mean to imply that the texts of the "Indian Cycle" rework or recount stories which have already taken place. The *fabula* or story is always eccentric to the frame of the *sjuzet* or narrative plot. Narrators are always pursuing events which took place long before they came on the scene to present us with their texts. Thus, the "Indian Cycle" is less a chronology than a tracking and a collage of what we can order into a chronology. The process by which these texts represent the past is less a representation, properly speaking, than an exhausting attempt at performing the past that leaves us feeling that the past is irretrievably and irresistibly past and has taken on a mythic patina. As the texts of the "Indian Cycle" persist in their tracking efforts to represent the past, we begin to lose our bearings on the original event that gave rise to so many repetitions and transformations.

Temporal disjunction between plot and story is not new; telling a story usually means that something has already happened. But the peculiarity of the temporal structure of the "Indian Cycle" lies in its equal insistence on the pastness of the past and on the desire of various characters to make that past present and visible. In the "Indian Cycle," temporal disjunction between story and plot is radical; so is the desire for a return to the past. The texts play this tension out both within themselves and between each other, by using each other as echoes and points of reference, by repeating, returning to, and circling around events. Finally, this peculiar fracturing of a story and its telling in different texts makes it most difficult to discern any coherent chronology.

The radical separation of event and narration and the ensuing temporal and spatial dislocation which characterize the texts and their relationship in the "Indian Cycle" is performed in an exemplary fashion in the film, *India Song*. The sound track is off. *Off* means that the source of the sound is not seen *on* the screen. From where are the disembodied voices speaking? What we see is studded with visual clues so that we begin to read the visuals as a past that is already being remembered but not represented. The film, to which I will return, leads us to ask questions about how we read film and text, how two semiotic systems, a visual and a linguistic, can work together. I suggest that *India Song* separates and doubles semiotic networks. This separation and doubling in the "Indian Cycle" can be addressed by the psychoanalytic model of fantasy.

Freud began studying fantasies at the end of the nineteenth century, in the context of the study of hysteria. Numbers of female patients came to him with problems that were generally called

35

hysteria—recurrent hallucinations or daydreams and inexplicable paralyses or other physiological phenomena among them. When analyzed, all symptoms pointed to traumatic sexual origins. This discovery led Freud to believe, initially, that his patients had all been sexually abused. The blame was placed at the family's door since most patients remembered that they had been abused by close family relatives—fathers, uncles, brothers. But Freud's thinking on the matter evolved. He eventually disavowed the unbearable reality of widespread paternal abuse, for reasons he describes in his letters to his friend Wilhelm Fliess, and shifted the blame, as it were, to the patients' sexual desires. He discovered infantile sexuality and the unconscious. He forged his infamous version of the seduction theory in which he considers that the patients' sexual desires are re-pressed but reemerge in fantasies which are imagined sexual scenes, imagined seductions.

Two contemporary French researchers, Laplanche and Pon-talis, have traced Freud's work on fantasy ("Fantasme"). Following their definition, fantasies are "scripts of organized scenes which are capable of dramatization—usually in a visual form. The subject is invariably present in these scenes . . . as an observer . . . [and] as a participant. . . ."[3] The function of fantasy, they argue, is to stage desire. Central to their definition is this two-part struc-ture—a visualization and a script organized in a sequence of scenes. Fantasy is a cinema of desire in which the spectator is cast as part of the spectacle.

Fantasy is about looking from and for a place. This place, I suggest, is what Lacan would describe as the place of the subject. This is an imaginary place in which conscious and unconscious desire coincide. Lacan's great contribution to psychoanalytic theory is his grafting of linguistic theory and Freud's psychoanalytic theory. Language situates us in the world. So does vision. Fantasy is a story about the displaced subject whose story is cast in two ways, in language and in visual perspective. Perspective organizes space. We usually interpret the ordering of space by one-point per-spective as a realistic representation of human vision and, therefore, as a description of a spectator's point of view. Perspective, then, would seem to describe the situation of the spectator. But this place of the subject, as described in single point perspective, is an impossible place. It appears to be a focal point from which every-thing is ordered, and which defines the vanishing point at which everything converges. But this spatial ordering does not really correspond to human vision. Our vision is not static. Our eye ranges over a visual field and we move, at different times, through the described space. Our vision is not monocular, but binocular. Debates on perspective in the visual arts are far-ranging. But it is fair to say that within the system of one-point perspective, the system which we assume represents human sight, the place of the subject proves once more to be virtual rather than visual. It represents an imaginary coherence and is therefore—and some would argue necessarily—a misrepresentation of itself.

Le Ravissement de Lol V. Stein, whose fascinating heroine has been displaced by a traumatic event and whose narrator, like a psychoanalyst, insists on describing the trauma in an appropriate and appropriating narrative frame, is an exemplary fantasy text. Lol makes numbers of exhausting attempts to bring the traumatic scene into full view. But narrative attempts to bring Lol's scene into the regulatory purview of language fail to recenter the subject.

A brief synopsis will be useful here for those unfamiliar with this novel. As a young girl, Lol Stein was jilted by her fiancé, Michael Richardson. The scene of her undoing is a summer dance, held in the local casino. A foreign femme fatale, Stretter, glides into the casino and sweeps Richardson off his feet. Forgotten by Richardson, Lol watches, immobilized, as he dances with Stretter. She is fascinated by the architecture of desire created by the glances of the characters. At dawn, the dance ends. Richardson and Stretter leave together. Upon losing sight of the couple, Lol loses consciousness, ravished by the scene of her own substitution.

Lol eventually marries, has children, and meets the narrator. This meeting, ten years after the crucial ball scene, establishes the temporal frame of the novel. When Lol meets him, the narrator is the lover of her childhood friend, Tatiana Karl, who had been at the ball with Lol. Tatiana was a fourth pair of eyes in the casino, observing the ricochet of glances. Lol seduces the narrator, but not before she reestablishes the triangle by which she was undone. Lol redistributes the roles of the various players. *She* is now the "other woman" and supplants Tatiana. One woman takes the place of another with respect to one man, and this substitution is visually acknowledged. The triangle is defined in terms of vision. The places in the triangle are determined as *seen* and *being seen*. The substitution results from being given to be seen. Lol orchestrates these performances in

37

scenes which recall the original seduction scene/seen. The narrator's fictionalization of the ball scene that opened the novel established the ball scene as the model for these subsequent repetitions. It is the absent referent, the scene that performance and narrations reiterate and strain to represent and which, like early trauma, returns to structure the present.

Le Ravissement de Lol V. Stein is ordered by a number of frame-ups. Architectural frames abound. As Lol arranges the other characters for visual consumption, she situates them in doorways, in window frames, or in the center of her field of vision. Her lover, the narrator Jacques Hold, will bring his lover, Tatiana, to the window of the hotel in which they rendezvous so that Lol, lying in a field near their hotel, can see her. All of these scenes reiterate the formal framing of the scene that originally displaced Lol and which now constitutes her daily fantasmatic cinema. Lol's fantasy cinema replays a version of the ball scene which repeats her dislocation. This simple repetition is, however, not so simple. Lol's scenario repeats her gaze—she sees the treacherous and enraptured couple—but it elides the gazes that set her in her place as displaced. Because Lol does not see herself seen, she repeats the scene which elides her place as the center of others' looks. Out of sight, Lol loses her sites. This is the sense of her loss of consciousness once Stretter and Richardson exit. Lol is pure vision. So long as she sees, she is conscious. Once, however, the object of her sight eludes her, she is subverted because vision, here, is the equivalent of "subject."

Lol is difficult to define and to captivate. She thwarts the narrator's efforts to write himself into her scenario. He can never take place in what has already occurred. All scenes subsequent to the fantasy of the ball scene bear the mark of the already seen. That past scene is never domesticated by a revisionist script because the script repeats Lol's blindness: Lol can never be represented. Because this gaze refuses to acknowledge that it is situated by the gazes of others, Lol is lost, like some modern Eurydice.

If *Le Ravissement de Lol V. Stein* performs the disjunction of vision and script, the reversal of this disjunction in *India Song* does no more to reunite sight and sound. The dominant visuals of the film and the displaced sound track of the "off" voices maintain and further complicate the split between sight and sound, between literature and cinema.

In *India Song* the reader discovers Stretter and Richardson living unhappily ever after in Calcutta. Their story is "told" by the disembodied voices who share the sound track with rumbas from the thirties. The voices recall the night of Lol's ravishing and recount that Richardson followed Stretter to Calcutta where she is the wife of the French ambassador. Stretter and Richardson are openly lovers; we see them in sensual, intimate poses. They seem to enjoy the complete indulgence of the Consulate. While we only see those actors we take to be these characters at a ball or at an elegant hotel, we learn, from the sound track, that Stretter drowned herself and Richardson became a maritime insurance salesman. The lovers' passion ends in the sweltering world of colonial India, but it has taken on mythic proportions. The off-screen voices speak of it in hushed tones; we understand that this story continues to fascinate those who would give voice to it.

This synopsis greatly simplifies the skewed scenic syntax of the film. The camera eye stares fixedly into a mirrored room for about one-third of the film. The angle of the camera, the reflection of light, and the play of the visual and virtual spaces which we see and do not understand until later, if at all, confuse us. However, *India Song* is fascinating. We are glued to the visuals as they play out the fantasy of vision and desire. We see characters pass through the space of the mirrored room and beyond. Because of the mirror, we see them before they enter the room, and when they pass in front of the mirror, we see them doubled. We see the characters as they watch themselves, as they watch each other, as they watch reflections of each other. We watch reflections of them watching each other in the mirror. We watch the characters silently revolve around Stretter as she seduces the men and as she loves Richardson. *India Song* plays with us as we watch desire played out in vision.

Because what we see and what we hear are so peculiarly linked, the here/now experience which we usually associate with going to the movies becomes an odd here/then disruption. We have to read what we see *now* as a *then*. We are given a variety of clues for this reading. For example, the second shot of the film shows a dark room in which an Indian servant lights a lamp on a piano and then recedes left to light two lamps flanking a mirror. He disappears left, and the camera pans the dark room, giving us the impression that it is an altar erected to the figure framed in the photograph on the piano.

A second example of this confusion of temporal frames is the

setting itself. The film was shot on location in France, in a dilapi-
dated chateau. When we see the façade, it is in ruins. We may want
to understand this building as the French Embassy, but it can only
be an embassy at some time that is not the present of the story. The
characters, when we finally see them, are dressed in Yves-Saint
Laurent renditions of chic thirties attire. We begin to get the picture.
What we are watching is not a representation but a self-conscious
performance stamped with the mark of the past. When the actress,
Delphine Seyrig, later looks at the photo on the piano, the unlike-
ness between actress and photo is evident and melancholic. We can
interpret these clues and understand that Duras wants to deny that
Delphine Seyrig is the diaphanous Stretter. Duras has her cast listen
to the recorded sound track; this, too, inflects their gestures with an
oneiric slowness. The entire visual film is marked by the disjunction
between seen and heard that characterizes the film's production.

Like *Le Ravissement de Lol V. Stein, India Song* stages desire. The framing devices of the novel are in evidence here. The film
is, of course, projected onto a screen. The mirrors repeat the frame
but play with the space represented. We see reflections which allow
us to see more than what the camera can frame. We understand the
limits of the frame, but we mistrust what we see indirectly, in the
mirror. Characters and details which we have come to understand as
already past are offered to us in mirrors, in frames, and in doorways
and windows. But we have learned to separate what we see and
what we know. *India Song*, like *Le Ravissement de Lol V. Stein,*
separates visual and linguistic information networks. But it goes
even further. It undermines our ability to read what we see. We
must learn to read differently, to read as if what we see is memory
and virtual, rather than a representation and simply visual.

India Song is a visionary film whose space is articulated by
glances and perceived visually. These are not simple direct glances,
but refracted, diverted, and deferred looks which repeat the problem
laid out in *Le Ravissement de Lol V. Stein*. Looks are not reciprocal. They issue from a point that articulates space but elides the
reciprocal glance which defines the place of the subject. Vision is
split, argues Lacan, between the subject and the object seen. What
we see is not what sees us, and it is what sees us which tells us who
we are. *India Song* plays with the play of vision. The space in
which this play is elaborated is a fantasy space.

The fantasy model is useful because it helps us theorize about the tension between seen and known and between the syntax of language and the language of vision. It also raises the possibility of using a more traditionally pictorial sign, perspective, as a tool with which we can approach the notion of the subject. In both cases, it raises the issue of the relationship between semiotic systems of representation. While it is not my intention to argue that fantasy is dominated by a linguistic model of signification, I would suggest this as an appropriate direction to take in later discussions. I hope to have shown that fantasy is a valuable model for approaching and describing the trajectory between the two endpoints of Marguerite Duras's "Indian Cycle," the inaugural novel, *Le Ravissement de Lol V. Stein,* and the penultimate film in the group, *India Song.*

NOTES

[1] For the official program of the summer film festival, see *Focus,* 1, No. 7 (1981).

[2] Marie-Claire Ropars-Wuilleumier, "La mort des miroirs: *India Song*—Son Nom de Vénise dans Calcutta désert," *L'Avant-Scène du Cinéma* 225 (1979): 4–12.

[3] Jean Laplanche and J.B. Pontalis, *The Language of Psychoanalysis,* trans. Donald Nicholson-Smith (New York: Norton, 1973) 318.

5. CINEMATOGRAPHY IN *THE MOVIEGOER*

Lewis A. Lawson

WALKER PERCY'S FIRST published novel, *The Moviegoer* (1961),[1] is set mainly in New Orleans and covers eight days in 1960 —from Wednesday, February 24, to Ash Wednesday, March 2. During that time the narrator, John Bickerson "Binx" Bolling, goes to the movies four times: on the first Wednesday night he sees *Panic in the Streets* with Richard Widmark, on Thursday night an unidentified western, on Saturday night *Fort Dobbs* with Clint Walker, and on the following Monday night *The Young Philadelphians* with Paul Newman. No wonder Dr. Harvey R. Greenberg in *The Movies on Your Mind* cites Binx Bolling to describe a type:

> One encounters chronic moviemania in rigid, inhibited types who feel exquisitely uncomfortable when forced into close interpersonal contact. Safe only in well-defined social situations, intolerably anxious if called upon to improvise, these people sleepwalk through the day's routine and only come alive at second hand, as proxy participants in the adventures of their idols. Walker Percy's elegant novel, *The Moviegoer*, describes such a case.[2]

Dr. Greenberg's generalization about moviemania may be

right, but he is doubly wrong about Binx Bolling. Greenberg is interested in what is typical, rather than individual, about Binx's moviegoing. He therefore focuses on the response that Binx makes to filmic reality, the movie product, but ignores Binx's response to cinematography, the movie process behind the filmic reality. Dr. Greenberg himself is thus typical of the critics.

During the day Binx is a stockbroker. He is very good at it, though he is not interested in it. Consequently he frequently pretends to be reading stock market reports, when he is, in fact, reading *Arabia Deserta*, concealed in a *Standard and Poor's* binder. *Arabia Deserta,* reissued with much success in 1955, is C. M. Doughty's classic account of his travels in disguise among the Bedouins. It is the only book that Binx owns or, apparently, has read in five years; reading it is Binx's way of reducing his life to an image, for he perceives himself as a disguised traveler in a world made desert by science. He calls this journey his "horizontal" search.

Binx recalls that he had once been a serious reader of "fundamental" books, weighty explanations of one subject or another, by such savants as Schroedinger, Einstein, Eddington, and Toynbee. Ultimately he reads a book entitled *The Chemistry of Life.* When he finishes it, he realizes that he has completed what he calls his "vertical" search. He then goes to the movies to see *It Happened One Night,* which, like *Arabia Deserta*, is a classic travel account. Binx has become both a disguised traveler and a moviegoer.

Binx's description of the "vertical" search is most revealing. He has in mind a picture of knowledge as a hierarchical system, with individual bits of sense data on the bottom and ever more inclusive categories of generalization as the ascent to the top is made. The description is ultimately Platonic: in *The Republic,* Plato uses the Analogy of the Sun, the Description of the Divided Line, and the Simile of the Cave to propound his system of education.[3] To take the last first, Plato describes a group of men who are held captive in a cave, whose world consists only of the shadows cast on the wall by an unseen fire. They are, in other words, caught up in matter, accepting as real not the essence but the appearance of a thing. Then one captive is taken out of the cave, allowed to see—by the light of the sun—things as they really are. Although he wishes to remain on such an elevated plane, he must return to tell his fellow captives of their mistaken belief that the shadows are real. He is the Philosopher-King who is supposed to rule justly because he has no selfish desire for the job but rules from a sense of duty. (Binx's Aunt Emily imagines herself to be the Philosopher-King.)

The Description of the Divided Line is an abstract repetition of the meaning of the Cave Simile: at the bottom of a vertical line is the Realm of Appearances, consisting of images and simple percepts; at the top of the line is the Realm of Intelligibles, consisting of mathematics, the Forms of Things, and the Idea of Truth. Thus Plato distinguishes between the ordinary world that anybody can see and the really important, *secret* world that only initiates, using technique, can apprehend. Plato's Simile of the Cave continues to be one of the most potent images in Western culture. It confidently asserts a progressive history for humankind, from the prehistoric cave man to the contemporary cosmic man. (Of course Binx's father, fascinated by 1930's science, took his son to see the tableau of Stone Age Man in Chicago's Field Museum.)

Modern physics has been much infatuated with the Simile of the Cave. Such writers as Pierre Duhem, Sir Arthur Eddington, Sir James Jeans, Werner Heisenberg, Sir Charles Sherrington, Erwin Schroedinger, Otto Frisch, and Carl Friedrich von Weizsäcker have pictured the physicist as the Platonic man who sees beyond the wall. Their image of the physicist is that of the priest who has penetrated the phenomena of locality and duration, to discover the mathematical truths that constitute a higher reality. Such men provide the books for the "vertical" search.

Other modern thinkers have seen the likeness of wall-watching to moviegoing. Henri Bergson, in *Creative Evolution* (1907), is the earliest writer I discovered to perceive the similarity. Thereafter, perhaps in debt to Bergson, a succession of French film historians and critics have rather superficially cited the Simile as a prophecy of cinematography. Since Binx is an avid moviegoer, it is quite possible that he has at sometime read some book on film that proudly notes the parentage of the cinema.

Another notice of the resemblance of moviegoing to wall-watching occurred in the English-speaking world. In his highly popular *Study of History,* another of Binx's influences, Arnold Toynbee, declares that if Plato were writing today he would use movie-watching as a substitute for the "elaborate and inevitably somewhat bizarre fantasy" of the Cave. And Francis M. Cornford, in his acclaimed edition of *The Republic,* just a few years later, independently makes the same comparison.

44

Thus, apparently unaware of its use by other disciplines, physicists, historians, philosophers, and film critics have employed the Simile of the Cave. But Binx Bolling has apparently read them all. By choosing the image of the moviegoer for himself, Binx announces that he perceives the triple resemblance: Plato's enlightened wall-watcher (that is, the Idealist philosopher) equals the modern physicist equals the moviegoer.

As a moviegoer (that is, Platonist-physicist) Binx should accept the basic distinction between the apparent and the Real. He should therefore sense a distinction between Space and Time, as they are presented on the screen, and place and duration, as he experiences them in his individual seat. In Platonic terms, Space and Time have Being (they are universal and eternal), place and duration are Becoming (they are local and transitory).

As a consequence of knowing the basic distinction regarding Space/place and Time/duration, the enlightened Binx presumably goes to the movies to admire the superior Space and Time Realities that cinematography presents.[4]

About Space Binx says, "Nowadays when a person lives somewhere, in a neighborhood, the place is not certified for him. More than likely he will live there sadly, and the emptiness which is inside him will expand until it evacuates the entire neighborhood. But if he sees a movie which shows his very neighborhood, it becomes possible for him to live, for a time at least, as a person who is Somewhere and not Anywhere"(63). Notice that Binx properly uses "place" to refer to his locale.

There are, as Sesonske has pointed out in a very thoughtful essay,[5] certain telling distinctions between "Ordinary space" (what I am calling "place") and "cinema space." "Ordinary space" is both continuous in three dimensions and affected by innate characteristics. That is to say, points in "ordinary space" are fixed, and one must pass through every intervening point to go from one point to another; there are no film cuts in real life. Moreover, the progress from one point to another is affected by all of the peculiarities of each locale; there is no isolation from the environment. "Cinema space," on the other hand, is wholly visual but dual in its visual presentation in that it has both "frame space" and "action space." "Frame space" is two-dimensional restriction placed upon the view. "Action space" is discontinuous both with "ordinary space" and within itself. The viewer can never get any closer to the presentation

45

by moving forward; action-sequence can be telescoped by cutting, and action-relation can be affected by lens manipulation. "Cinema space" is a distortion of "ordinary space" by technology, yet is highly preferable, in that it transcends such ordinary experiences as tedium, the sense of the irrelevant, and the sense of clutter, in short, what Binx calls "everydayness." When he goes to see *Panic in the Streets,* the New Orleans locale, in which he actually lives, is the setting. Triumphantly, he says that "certification" has taken place. In other words, vast amounts of "ordinary space" have been collected and reduced by the cinematographical process to a single set of images that possesses greater clarity, isolation of purpose, and meaning.

Time, too, is different. "Ordinary time" is genuine linearity; there are no discontinuous moments; each moment of slow change depends upon all previous moments. Most moments are not really all that perfect; they are so everyday that an individual tries to ignore their boring presence by dwelling in the future (that is, the perfect possible) or the past (that is, an artificial story which has had all the everydayness edited out of it). Thus the individual spurns his present, yet is depressed when it goes away unwanted. Biologically considered, time can only be evidence of entropy.

"Cinema time" is quite different. In the first place it is universal. Binx says that before he can enter a theater, he must talk with the manager or ticket seller; for, otherwise, he says, "I should be lost, cut loose metaphysically speaking. I should be seeing one copy of a film which might be shown anywhere and at any time. There is a danger of slipping clean out of space and time. It is possible to become a ghost and not know whether one is in downtown Loews in Denver or suburban Bijou in Jacksonville" (75).

Second, a movie, carefully composed of a beginning, middle, and ending, can eternally recur. "Cinema time" is cyclical; it *re*volves, whereas "ordinary time" *e*volves. It is doctored, consisting of selected stills spliced together to present a meaningful pattern. On Thursday, Binx goes to see a western, to experience not just the filmic action but the cinematographical experience that he calls "repetition." A "repetition" is an isolated time segment from which the stuff of actual experience has been removed; a "repetition" is, as Binx says, "time itself, like a yard of smooth peanut brittle" (80). Fourteen years before, he had seen another western in the same theater. What happens this time? The westerns (their specificity

46

submerged in a type) *be,* there is no change in them; yet the theater seats have *become* more scarred and beaten up. Even so, the seats *endure*, offering a clue that Binx vows to follow.

There are yet other characteristics of cinematographic time (and remember, we are speaking of scientific time). A unit of process time, as opposed to filmic time, is unvarying—so many frames per second. Process time thus becomes spatialized by uniformity, loses its pulsating human characteristic, and can be measured by quantity rather than quality. The screen thus becomes the moving image of Eternity, as Plato defines Time in the *Timaeus*.

A final word about "cinema time." The cinematographical process must go in one direction. Even if the pattern of filmic images is reversed, the process itself is nevertheless going forward, always rolling off a reel, going through a projector, and then rolling onto another reel. The reversal of film direction (as opposed to filmic action) simply defies our sense of the logical. Hence the physicists have been fond of the movie projector image when they discuss what Eddington termed "time's arrow," the definition of time as movement in a certain direction, in a condition of entropy, from organization toward disorganization, from heat toward its dissipation.[6] Thus, science envisions a time when time must have a stop, when it is all rolled up on the second reel, when the universe has become a dead cinder.

Cinematography, then, conveys to Binx a set of statements about his placement in the world. The screen represents a higher reality than he can experience himself. Hence it can, as in *Panic in the Streets*, certify his ghostly actuality. But the certification quickly loses its effectiveness, and he is once again alienated from that wondrous realm.

Suffering from such everydayness, he attempts to employ repetitions, to collapse the fourteen years between westerns into a meaningful pattern by discarding the dross and splicing together the significant moments. At the same time, he attempts to live as the desert traveler, open to all novelty and always moving on, without being affected by the environment. This kind of spectator's life is certified for him on Saturday night when he goes to see *Fort Dobbs*. "Clint Walker rides over the badlands, up a butte, and stops. He dismounts, squats, sucks a piece of mesquite, and studies the terrain. A few decrepit buildings huddle down there in the canyon. We know nothing of him, where he comes from or where he goes"

(143). Clint Walker thus personifies rotation, the escape from the present by constant anticipation of the future. Binx is delighted with the sense of reality conferred on him by this certification, but it does not last, and he wakes up in the middle of the night "in the grip of everydayness."

Is there, then, no hope in the modern world for the person who is not satisfied to be a moviegoer, a worshipper of the split world proffered by science? There is, and ironically, the last movie to which Binx goes implies the answer. On Monday night, when he and Kate are in Chicago, they see *The Young Philadelphians*. Binx describes the plot: "Paul Newman is an idealistic young fellow who is disillusioned and becomes cynical and calculating. But in the end he recovers his ideals" (211). Binx is really foreshadowing his future, when *he* becomes the new man. But what is being pictured here? The title, *The Young Philadelphians,* gives it away. They are the young inhabitants of love. Following the Christian existentialists, Walker Percy believes that communion, intersubjectivity as Marcel calls it, is the basis of shared reality, the only alternative to the isolated reality offered by Plato and Descartes. Such a love is an incarnation, a blending of spirit with body.

We should be prepared, then, for the conclusion. In her majestic speech to Binx, Aunt Emily states that almost everyone is a Laodician, whom God will surely punish, now that the Apocalypse has come.[7] Fleeing from her despair and censure and losing faith in Kate, Binx imagines himself in Hell, covered with feces, finally swamped by dead matter, in the Last Days. Then Kate arrives, her action a proof of love, and Binx turns his attention to the neighboring church at which communicants are arriving for the daubing of ashes on Ash Wednesday. Earthly love is thus seen as a reflection of Divine Love. Kate and Binx are not Laodicians, but rather Philadelphians, citizens of that city which is complimented in Rev. 3:7 for its constancy. Binx has rejected the two realms of Plato to accept the two cities of St. Augustine.[8] There has been no Apocalypse after all, but time will go on as a mystery, and a human being must watch and wait in faith. Consequently, just like most other people, Binx gets married and stops going to movies.

NOTES

[1] Unless otherwise stated, the excerpts from *The Moviegoer* are quoted from Walker Percy, *The Moviegoer* (New York: Noonday Press, 1967).

[2] Harvey R. Greenberg, *The Movies on Your Mind* (New York: Saturday Review Press, 1975) 75. See Lewis A. Lawson, "Moviegoing in *The Moviegoer*," in *Walker Percy: Art and Ethics*, ed. Jac Tharpe (Jackson Press of Mississippi, 1980) 26–42.

[3] An explanation of the relationship between the cinema and the Cave is available (Lewis A. Lawson, "Walker Percy's *The Moviegoer:* The Cinema as Cave," *Southern Studies,* XIX [1980]: 331–54).

[4] Further discussion of the Time/Space problem is available in Lewis A. Lawson, "Time and Eternity in *The Moviegoer*," *Southern Humanities Review,* 16 (1982): 129–41.

[5] Alexander Sesonske, "Cinema Space," in *Exploration in Phenomenology,* eds. David Carr and Edward S. Casey (The Hague: Martinus Nijhoff, 1973) 399–403.

[6] For example, consider Erwin Schroedinger's observation: "With very few exceptions (that really are exceptions) the course of events in nature is irreversible. If we try to imagine a time-sequence of phenomena exactly opposite to one that is actually observed—as in a cinema-film projected in reversed order—such a reversed sequence, though it can easily be imagined, would nearly always be in gross contradiction to well-established laws of physical science" *(Mind and Matter* [Cambridge: University Press, 1958] 83).

[7] Discussions of the role of Aunt Emily are available (Lewis A. Lawson, "William Alexander Percy, Walker Percy, and the Apocalypse," *Modern Age,* XXIV [Fall 1980]: 396–406, and "Walker Percy's Southern Stoic," *Southern Literary Journal,* III [Fall 1970]: 5–31).

[8] A tracing of the development of the novel from Plato to St. Augustine is available (Lewis A. Lawson, "The Allegory of the Cave and *The Moviegoer*," *South Carolina Review,* XIII [Spring 1981]: 13–18).

6. GENERIC TENSION IN *PSYCHO*

Paul Petlewski

PSYCHO IS GENERALLY characterized as an assault upon the viewer, and it is. It is also a tease. It teases by questioning some of the basic conventions of film narrative: coherence, consistency, the very nature of beginnings. Why, for instance, does a story center upon this character rather than that character? If *Psycho* can begin by promising us the story of Marion Crane (which turns out to be the end of her story and the middle of Norman Bates's story), then why not begin anywhere? What were the stories of those two young girls who apparently preceded Marion into the swamp? What was the story of the relationship between Mrs. Bates and her lover—and Norman?

These are questions which we ask only after the fact, after the movie, if at all. But *Psycho*, more than most films, invites us to consider them. Most films, after all, do not produce large blocks of narrative which apparently exist not to reveal but to conceal the privileged story (Norman's story) or, more exactly, the nature of the privileged story. And yet if the first third of *Psycho* (the Marion story) exists primarily to betray audience expectations, the other two-thirds (with their pattern of investigation/danger, another investigation/more danger) take some pains to fulfill them.

Psycho is centrally concerned with concealment, and it begins by disguising its interest in disguise. The first half hour suggests that it is to be grounded in a realist aesthetic, like *The Wrong Man*, a kind of semi-documentary crime story. Some explicit cinematic signals supporting this occur immediately, as titles establish a particular

50

city, day, date, and time. The fact that it is December 11 has no dramatic relevance whatsoever, and the day and time (which do have narrative significance) could easily be conveyed by less insistent methods. But by literally foregrounding this information, *Psycho* attempts to validate its status as history and as truth; it certifies its own credentials as deliberately as the opening of an evening newscast. When the flat black-and-white photography, conventional camera set-ups, and use of location work (locations which will gradually be usurped by studio sets) are added to this foregrounding, the film seems to promise something resembling a criminal procedure. The narrative will establish the motivation leading up to a relatively conventional crime (indeed, by cinematic standards a very dull crime) and will trace the *logical* consequences of that crime— namely, those consequences which can be contained by the premises of the genre.

There are other devices, primarily narrative, which work to suggest gritty realism. The characters are placed within a fairly precise socio-economic background (witness the drab hotel room for the afternoon assignation). More important, they are provided with motivation (debt, divorce, alimony payments, possible loneliness, even desperation) which we accept as mundane, commonplace, the stuff of ordinary life. Psychological background and sheer accident (the sudden availability of $40,000) combine to create a context in which theft becomes plausible, even reasonable.

Now the semi-documentary mode exists primarily as process, as explication—how things work, how things happen. When utilized within the crime story, the mode tends to document how people go bad and how things go wrong. It offers openness, revelation; the camera will show all that is important and a lot (like December 11) that is unimportant. It also emphasizes a surface comprehensiveness in its treatment of minor characters, all of whom are given individualizing quirks (the boss keeps a bottle in his desk, a secretary takes tranquilizers on her wedding day) which are meant to evoke real people, people whose lives continue beyond the limits of the frame. In other words, the first third of *Psycho* insists that it is interested in the constant revelation of truth. As Marion drives off to Fairvale, the questions generated by the narrative are firmly based on this assumption. Durgnat has suggested the nature of the plot complications anticipated by the audience: "the theft won't be noticed until Monday morning, she can always return the money. Will

51

she go on to decide to return it, but lose it? Will someone else steal it from her? Will Sam betray her, by his weakness, somehow?"[1] At this point the audience may be uneasy about the eventual fate of Marion but not about the nature of the film they are watching.

But then Marion sees a flickering neon sign—and she drives out of the crime movie into what appears to be a horror movie, into melodrama, certainly into a different world than the one which has been occupying the screen. Normally, different "worlds" in films are clearly defined and differentiated, as in a *Wizard of Oz* or a *Time Machine;* they do not get confused. But part of the peculiarity of *Psycho* (and perhaps one of the reasons that it produces such uneasiness in spectators) is that a slippage keeps occurring. The film refuses to anchor itself firmly in any one genre. It keeps sending up conflicting signals as radically different conventions and styles fight for possession of the frame.

Consider, for instance, the way in which the realist crime story suddenly collides with the iconography of the Gothic horror film. On the one hand, there is the motel— realistic enough, small, cheap, a bit run down—a motel that would not seem out of place in a film like *They Live by Night*. On the other hand, there is the Bates house, perched up on a hill. Hitchcock has defended that house, with a straight face, on the grounds of verisimilitude. He is even quoted as saying, "I did not set out to reconstruct an old-fashioned Universal horror-picture atmosphere."[2] But the evidence on the screen flatly contradicts his statement. In terms of framing (low angles) and atmospheric effects (driving rain, a mysterious figure silhouetted in the window, dark clouds scudding overhead), this is clearly an Old Dark House; James Whale could have been proud of it.

In fact, the intermittent "Gothicizing" of *Psycho* begins within the motel itself. That nondescript structure is suddenly revealed as a halfway house which serves to join the two worlds. Norman's office (with its desk, ashtray, keys on the wall), is, at best, functional; it goes unnoticed. But the parlor belongs to the world of the house, with its overflow of stuffed birds casting ominous shadows *on the ceiling*. The fact that we are even aware of the ceiling indicates something else: within that parlor the film's visual style has begun to oscillate, utilizing different conventions to separate the two characters. Marion Crane is photographed in straightforward medium-closeups, the style that has dominated the film up to this point.

But Norman is sometimes photographed from an obtrusive low angle, an unsettling composition that eventually relegates him to the right of the frame while a particularly threatening stuffed bird, wings outstretched, appropriates the left of the frame.

This stylistic split continues, though more sporadically, throughout the shower murder, where the shots centering on Marion almost resemble cinema verité with their bright lighting, blurriness, and apparent haphazard quality of composition. Opposed to these are all the reverse shots of Norman-as-Mother, which look much more carefully composed and are, for obvious reasons, photographed with deliberate and astute use of heavy shadow. To these examples of the Gothic (all clustering around Norman) may be added a few additional items: Mother's corpse at the climax, the occasionally expressionistic lighting and camera angles, even the beginning of the shower murder itself (which has an analogue in the Val Lewton devil-cult film, *The Seventh Victim*).[3]

With the death of Marion we might expect the film to increase its use of horror film devices, but instead the reverse occurs. *Psycho* temporarily abandons the Gothic and returns to the conventions of the realist crime film, this time replacing Marion with Norman as the central figure. I am referring particularly to the sheer detail (dramatically insignificant detail) involved in Norman's cleaning-up operation. The camera watches patiently as Norman wraps the body, washes his hands, mops the tub, mops the floor, dries the walls, dries the floor, searches the room for evidence of Marion's presence, and so on. At this point *Psycho* is concentrating on a series of small, meticulous actions that do little to advance the narrative but which reassert the film's commitment to clinical documentary accuracy, to the impression that there is no detail too small for the camera to record.

Meanwhile, any other growing suspicions about the film's genuine interest in openness and revelation have been at least muted by providing us with both criminal and motivation: Mother has killed Marion in a fit of jealous rage. Indeed, all these gestures in the direction of realism seem powerful enough to prevent the viewer from being altogether disconcerted by the next Gothic item that puts in an appearance: a convenient swamp which serves as the burial ground for cars and bodies—at least four of each by the film's end.

Finally, though, these periodic references to the horror film relate to style rather than to story (nothing in the story, for instance, demands the Gothic nature of the Bates's house), and they are as deceptive about the film's real nature as the initial tendency towards realism has been. *Psycho* remains slippery and ambiguous because neither mode ever leaves the film entirely. The murder of Arbogast, some elaborate camera movement and cutting within the house, the chiaroscuro lighting effects when Mother is finally discovered, the final quick superimposition of Mother's face upon Norman's—all of these elements may be subsumed into the horror genre.

Similarly, the bows to realism continue in the film's second half, though with decreasing frequency. We note, for instance, the picture's total lack of interest in locating the viewer topographically, of suggesting where Fairvale is in relation to the motel, or where the motel is in relation to the swamp. They tend to coalesce around the figure of Arbogast, in four quick shots, as he visits hotels and boarding houses searching for Marion (echoing police procedures) and in his clever, practiced interrogation of Norman. Most of all, the nature of the performances maintains the veneer of realism. With the exception of John McIntire's crusty character bit as Sheriff Chambers (and possibly the presentation of Mother herself), all of the performances fall within a style of acting that can be identified as low-key or New York Naturalistic—a far cry from the heightened, more stylized performances associated with nonrealistic films.

While *Psycho* may begin in realism (and dabble with its trappings throughout), once Norman Bates has arrived, it becomes a different kind of picture. It becomes a classical detective story, not all that different from recent movies based upon Agatha Christie's novels. In fact, if Marion's murder were moved to the beginning of the film this would be glaringly apparent; we would have a work very much on the order of, say, *The Spiral Staircase*. What complicates *Psycho* from a generic aspect is the introduction and continuing use of the Gothic paraphernalia. This is not merely decorative or atmospheric; it seems to function as a bridge between the realist crime story and the classical detective story—a bridge and a disguise. For these horror elements are so instantly recognizable and carry such a powerful iconographic charge that they mask the shift that takes place and *keep* masking it. They work to disguise the fact that *Psycho* has abruptly switched genres.

An awareness of this switch, though, involves a reconsideration of the apparent premises of the film; the classical detective story employs narrative conventions which are exactly the opposite of those found in the realist crime story. It is not an exposé, a revelation, but an elaborate construct, a game based upon a deliberate strategy of deception. It is designed not to enlighten but to mislead the viewer, to offer false explanations, false suspects and to conceal truth—particularly the true "why" (motive) and the true "who" (criminal). The real causes of the crime are normally buried in the past (exactly the case here) and once they are revealed, the story ends. Indeed, the main oddity in the second half of *Psycho* is that, in terms of story as opposed to plot, the genre stands nakedly exposed; only the deceptive plot elements introduced in the first half prevent us from realizing that the film is awash with detectives (Arbogast, Sam, Lila, the sheriff, the true detective, the psychiatrist) and virtually bereft of suspects (Norman and Mother).

Perhaps this goes some way towards explaining the critical controversy that surrounds Dr. Richman, the psychiatrist. For if the film is considered as essentially realistic, then his explanation may well sound too smooth, too pat, insufficient to account for the experience we have endured. As the "final chapter" of the detective story, though—in which the detective is the magician, the god-figure who brings all that is hidden to light—his presence is more than appropriate; the film would be inconceivable without him.

This paper has considered three generic elements operating in *Psycho*. It has ignored at least two others: the black comedy and formal "Hitchcock film." Even suggesting the presence of additional elements complicates matters more, renews the question, "Just what kind of movie is this?" *Psycho* turns out to be a chameleon film, constantly changing, shifting, adapting different coloration, form, style. It tests the limits of the genre film.

NOTES

[1] Raymond Durgnat, *The Strange Case of Alfred Hitchcock* (Cambridge, MA.: The MIT Press, 1974) 323.

[2] Francois Truffaut, *Hitchcock* (New York: Simon and Schuster, 1967) 205.

[3] Joel Siegel, *Val Lewton: The Reality of Terror* (New York: The Viking Press, 1973) 124.

7. AMBIGUITY AS SUBVERSION IN THE FILMS OF ROBERT ALDRICH

T. J. Ross

AS A POPULAR ARTIST, Robert Aldrich usually works within genre conventions. At the same time, in keeping with a familiar tendency in modernist literature and art, Aldrich's exercise in a particular form proves also to be an essay on that form. Ambiguities of tone and theme in his films arise from the interplay between obligatory action set-pieces and the marginal notations offered on such sequences in a running commentary that complicates or subverts plot formulas and stock images. It is with ambiguities of character of a kind which serves to challenge stock responses and to complicate the action that I will be chiefly concerned in these remarks.

A standard scene in war movies, for example, shows the browbeating interrogation of Allied soldiers by their captors. We arrive at such a moment in Aldrich's *Too Late the Hero,* a World War II saga set in the South Pacific, when a Japanese officer aims his pistol at the head of one of a group of prisoners while warning the others: "Tell me what I want to know, or I'll fire." As the men look away, an off-camera shot is heard. The prisoners begin babbling in unison when, turning around, they see that their compatriot has not been scratched. The officer's query—"Did you really think I would shoot this man?"—is as clearly directed at us in the audience as at the figures on screen, and we are caught as much off guard as they. Or we were, at any rate, in 1970, when the film was released, for the Hollywood image of the Japanese military, even as late as 1970, consisted of little more than a mass of indistinguishable creatures, flying their planes into battleships or clambering up and down trees—an indistinguishable mass, if you will, of Kamikazniks. The civilizing shock of perception dealt us by the officer's query blocks our conditioned response and modifies our attitude to the officer so that it remains, at the least, ambiguous. The officer in fact is shown to be the most cultivated man on either side. And though cultivated manners as the mask for sinister motives is a familiar gambit in action movies (as typified by the villain in blue suede shoes in Aldrich's own *Kiss Me Deadly*), in this instance, the officer's cultivation is seen to be a reinforcing aspect of his humanity, of a moral and emotional dimension the betrayal of which in the lust for survival is at the heart of this film's concerns.

In such films as *Kiss Me Deadly, Too Late the Hero,* or *The Grissom Gang,* Aldrich invites the objection that he goes too far in exploiting brutal or gross effects; yet the question of how far one may go before descending into a dehumanizing and self-defeating nihilism is precisely Aldrich's theme. There is a bottom line beyond which his protagonists will not be pushed. Thus the moment recurs through Aldrich's films when his hero tells off a nihilistic heavy with a verve that such a master of invective as, say, John Osborne would applaud. Anyone in the film world who had ever fantasized about telling off Louella or Hedda or Rona would be especially taken with the way the Kim Novak character in *The Legend of Lylah Clare* tells off the film's crippled, cane-toting gossip columnist. In a similar manner, Jack Palance plays a beleaguered actor who lays into the bullying producer played by Rod Steiger in *The Big Knife* —and also sounds off against a corrupt general in *Attack*. In snubbing a necessity of survival—in itself the prime motive of animals —the Aldrich hero resists being dehumanized. Though he may be destroyed, he attains a level of interest and appeal beyond the melodramatic.

Discussing the film version of *The Grapes of Wrath* in *Magic and Myth of the Movies,* Parker Tyler observed that a melodramatic situation is one solvable simply by the overcoming of physical obstacles.[1] Taking our cue from Tyler, we may note how Aldrich, in his quest for more complex levels of interest and assertion, presses melodramatic plot elements toward the grotesque and toward the sort of extreme situation in which moral and psychological pressures count in the reckoning. And the more such pressures are felt, the more ambiguities abound. In this respect, too, Aldrich's work reflects the modernist manner in style and approach.

In his *Too Late the Hero,* Aldrich deals with a British unit assigned to destroy an enemy radio station. The unit is joined by a gum-chewing American officer played by Cliff Robertson. Yanked into action from furlough, the American is in no dedicated or "gung-ho" mood. Neither, he finds, are any of the British team except for the commanding officer, a man as evidently courageous as he is self-serving, and whose indifference to the men in his command is never more evident than when he mutters, "Good luck, chaps." Unlike his Japanese counterpart, this officer does not hesitate to shoot a wounded captive; and he is himself slain when, bypassing orders, he leads a premature raid on the enemy station. His death is virtually assured when Robertson holds back from supporting him on his foray. In this film of combat, the members of the Allied team are seen to be mainly in combat among themselves, their deaths determined more by the decisions each makes about the other than by the enemy.

At the opposite end of the scale from the commanding officer is the group's plebeian, cowardly goldbrick, who is presented as no sort of Sgt. Schweik but rather as the sort who first slices the ring finger off of a dead Japanese and then, to save his own neck, cuts the throat of another member of his squad. When his time comes, he dies the ugliest death of the group, disembowelled and strung upside-down on a tree. When troops desert and are taken by the enemy, not a moment's thought is given by their former mates to effecting their rescue.

We are surely a long way here from the kind of team spirit, ethnic ecumenicalism, and buddy-buddy romance celebrated in the usual war movie. Between the officers and troops there is mutual, class-conscious disdain; and there is little sign of fellow-feeling among the officers themselves or among the men in the ranks. Rather, the prevailing ethos is every man for himself. This applies as well to the more passive men in the group, who follow the line of least resistance, whether ordered about by the tight-lipped officer or the vituperative goldbrick.

Cliff Robertson's peer in the action is co-star Michael Caine, who plays the unit's medic. For both himself and the men in his care, he maintains, as befits a Michael Caine, a touchy sense of dignity. This puts him at odds with the commanding officer whom, to be sure, he finds occasion to tell off, launching into a "what-are-we-doing-here-anyway?" speech of a kind that was common in World War I films. It is uttered in a film as early as *The Big Parade,* sounded again in *All Quiet on the Western Front,* but it was rarely to be heard in World War II movies and so strikes a further edgy note.

In the climactic sequence, Robertson, who had refused to back the commanding officer in a risk beyond the bounds of duty, compels Caine to join him in such a risk by running across an open field in view of the enemy to an Allied camp posted out of range of the enemy artillery. In contrast to the British officer who seeks to regain prestige lost on an earlier failed mission, Robertson's action seems based finally on an acknowledgment of an imperative beyond self. The gum-chewing American turns out to be the one who insists on recognizing the collective interest by taking with him the decent but adamantly self-enclosed Englishman on the run to the British base to bring news of a hidden enemy airfield.

As the two set off, with bullets zinging around, the men at the base cheer them on, very much like a crowd egging on a player trying to steal home from third. In the next shot however, the camera pulls back to an angle high overhead, which adds to our suspense. We will be unable to tell which one may be brought down or which one makes it. The changed perspective also makes the men appear as tiny as insects scurrying across a landscape. Bullets put a sting in their tails, so to speak, even as in an earlier image some of the troops had been shown setting a pair of cockroaches in a race across a circled patch of ground by hotfooting them with the burning tips of their cigarettes, all the while cheering them on.

In the climactic sequence, the recall of the roach race does not evoke the kind of exact (and simplistic) equation that would wholly undercut the valor of the run. Nor does the absurdist-sports image serve to negate the effect of the action, an effect I have heard described as "shattering" by those seeing the film for the first time. The animalistic and the absurdist are subsumed, rather, in what remains (however double-edged) a humanist assertion. In the film's closing ambiguous shot, we are left to add up the score for ourselves as we behold the character we had seen stretched languorously on the sands of a beach in the film's opening shot, this time slumped dead on the camp ground. Others circle around him, including the hero, who despite himself has been reintegrated with the group by bringing home the message, and as the camera pulls back, he is virtually lost in the group.

The script for *Too Late the Hero* was originally co-authored by Aldrich and given final shape by Lukas Hellar. The film remains one of Aldrich's most characteristic and powerful works. Like other Aldrich films—*Kiss Me Deadly,* for example, or *The Grissom Gang* —*Too Late the Hero* received cool reviews and scant attendance. Aldrich rarely refers to it in his interviews and is rarely asked to. In its ambiguous approach to the individual and the collective, and in the more pessimistic Conrad-like aspects that would inhere in such an approach, *Too Late the Hero* was unlikely to appeal to the mood of the early seventies: a mood keyed to films with a more clearly defined ideological thrust.

In various films Aldrich has concentrated on pairs like the Robertson-Caine tandem, in which one involves himself in the fate of other individuals or groups, and the antinomian other remains imperiously aloof, while our responses ambiguously waver toward each. Such pairs include Gary Cooper and Burt Lancaster in *Vera Cruz;* Rock Hudson and Kirk Douglas in *The Last Sunset;* and Kim Novak opposite Peter Finch in *The Legend of Lylah Clare.*

One type of character for whom an Aldrich lead may find himself taking responsibility is exemplified by Joseph Cotten in *The Last Sunset,* who is greeted by the cry of "It's only Papa!" when we first behold him approaching the ranch house where his family awaits him. The cry takes on an ambiguous resonance indeed in a later scene when he is humiliated in a saloon, and it becomes painfully clear that the modifying "only" signifies not simply not-to-worry but a domestication so complete as to have proved unmanning. What saves him in the barroom scene is the intervention of the hero. Humiliation scenes are as much an Aldrich trademark as scenes of invective, and recurringly his heroes are faced with deciding how far to let things go before stepping in.

The plot of Aldrich's crime thriller of 1975, *Hustle,* chiefly turns on this question. In a role corresponding to Cotten's in *The Last Sunset,* Ben Johnson plays a hapless Papa desperate to learn the truth about his daughter who has disappeared into San Francisco's sex underground. The news of her violent death elicits one question from the police chief: "Is her father anybody?" to which detective Burt Reynolds reassuringly replies: "Nobody."

To Reynolds, "nobodies" are those who lack "juice." Among

those who may lack juice are the anonymous victims of criminal violence. In the opening sequence, Reynolds shoots it out with a thug holding as hostage a woman whom he contemptuously refers to as a "cow." The thug is brought down and the woman saved. But toward the end of the film, when Reynolds intercedes in a grocery store holdup, a woman bystander is shot and the hero himself slain. Ironically, the hero had been en route to the airport where he was to meet his love and embark with her for a new life in his dream city, Rome. Both confrontations with wild-eyed thugs leave us, in their contrasting effects, with a more ambiguous perspective on the problems posed by such head-on shoot-outs than is allowed for in the super-vigilante heroics of a Dirty Harry or indeed of the character played by Reynolds (in a virtual replay of his role in *Hustle)* in the recent *Sharkey's Machine,* a film which so glumly adheres to formula that it further adds to our appreciation of the Aldrich film.

In both *Sharkey's Machine* and *Hustle,* the heroines hustle as high-priced call girls. But just as the hero of the Aldrich film is seen as something more than a monstrous superboy, so too, the heroine, given the ambiguous edge in her characterization, is presented as something more than the comic-book Wonder Woman we find in *Sharkey's Machine.* Aldrich gains depth and believability for his heroine by eschewing not only an antiquated heart-of-gold standard but also—in contrast to what Reynolds caters to in *Sharkey's Machine—* an oversimplified knee-jerk feminism. Thus his heroine, though capably self-sufficient, openly seeks, in fact insists on the hero's avowal of "care" and, further, his avowal to "care for" her.

That Aldrich is to a self-conscious degree sensitive to the question of how far one may go in one's play on genre conventions is evident in *Hustle* in the cross-references to other films spotted through it. In the coda that follows the death of the hero, we observe heroine Catherine Deneuve waiting for him at the airport until she is met by his partner with the news that causes her to lean numbly on her informant as he leads her back to the hustling streets.

Earlier in the film, Deneuve and Reynolds had been shown at the movies, where, over their shoulders, we watch with them the concluding shot of Claude Lelouch's *A Man and a Woman.* In this shot, parted lovers (one of them played by Deneuve's peer in continental glamor, Anouk Aimee) enjoy an ecstatic reunion at a railway station; as the couple embrace, the theme song plays full blast on the sound track. Lelouch's film proved so popular on its

American release that Aldrich could depend on the scene's being recognized by a good number of his audience. And some in the audience might take note too of how the corresponding airport scene of *Hustle* spares us the schmaltz that Lelouch lays on with a trowel. Not that sad endings are necessarily "truer" than happy endings but that Aldrich's film is more apt in its moral and emotional coherence than the strictly commercial, if more pretentiously tricked-out fare represented by *A Man and a Woman*. By means of his nod at Lelouch, Aldrich asks us to recognize his own relative seriousness in his view of what is due to the audience, a matter he is as much concerned with in *Hustle,* as his hero is concerned with what is due to "nobodies."

On another occasion, when the lovers watch TV, we see flashed on the screen an excerpt from a film that Western buffs in the audience may recognize as a scene from *Branded,* a film directed by Aldrich's fellow specialist in action genres, Rudolph Maté. This more esoteric reference is more of an inside gag than the reference to *A Man and a Woman* but it works with a similar pressure of intent: *Branded's* hero, Alan Ladd, seeks, sure enough, to hustle an old rancher by posing as his long lost son. Complications set in when the rancher's daughter finds herself disturbingly drawn to her presumed brother. Things are at last set right when Ladd routs his partner in the hustle, finds the rancher's true heir, and joins the family as beloved son-in-law. In recalling *Branded,* with its stricken patriarch, missing child, and hustling intruders, Aldrich points up, of course, his own riskier and darker treatment of similar plot ingredients. And the incest theme with which *Branded* flirts not only reminds us of the greater dramatic force with which incest is treated in Aldrich's Western, *The Last Sunset,* where it is central to the plot, but also alerts us to the incestuous shadings in the characterization of the father in *Hustle*.

We also see on the TV screen a shot from Huston's *Moby Dick* of Ahab's fight with the great white whale, which points to Aldrich's own ultimate concern, beyond the surface play of cops and robbers, with the recognition of and response to the force of evil. Burt Reynold's way of responding in *Hustle* is to overstep legal bounds in order to save the anguished and "juiceless" Ben Johnson. When asked his reason for going so far, Reynolds says, "Sometimes you've got to try to turn the wheel around."

In Aldrich's best-known film, *Kiss Me Deadly,* we enter a

scene all the more stark for seeming to contain no character interested in turning the wheel around. Yet the film's lines of moral conflict are clearly established from the start, marked out by the brutish protagonist's theme song—"What's in it for me?"—and the coded behest to him of the film's first victim: "remember me." The conflict, then, is of a kind we have noted in the other films and the treatment as ambiguous, if harsher. Thus the nastier a character's motives, the more polite his moves. "Give him some of that sincerity," says Mike to Velda as he sends her off to hustle a client. "Be polite," says archvillain Dr. Soberin as he sends an underling to sound out Hammer.

If in his invectives an Aldrich character can sound like someone out of an Osborne play, the characters of the more muted world of *Kiss Me Deadly* (where only the villain is notably articulate) seem closer to Pinter in their ominously polite exchanges:

> —The police have already been through her
> apartment.
> —She told yuh, the police have already been through
> her apartment.
> —I know, the police have already been through this
> apartment.

As to the large dosage of violence in *Kiss Me Deadly,* it marks the continuation of negotiations by other means, and, wholly in contrast to the hysterically personal conniptions of Mickey Spillane's hero, no character in the film, least of all its hero, is personally motivated in his violence. And acts of violence prove all the more sadistic for being impersonal and businesslike in motive.

The action of the film is punctuated by a series of screams, beginning with the screams of its first victim, Christine, under torture. Next is Nick, a mechanic, who dreams of owning a white sports car, and who screams in terror when the lift of a car he has been lying under is released and he is crushed beneath the car's weight. Later, a venal morgue attendant, who had been holding his hand out to Hammer for more bribe money, screams when his impatient interlocutor slams a desk drawer shut on his hand. And when the villainess finds the box—"the Great Whatsit"—that she had sought and killed for and opens it despite being warned that to do so would "let loose all the evil in the world," her scream proves to be the climactic one, as she is engulfed by a great white atomic flame.

The obsessively materialistic pursuits of the characters boomerang with a vengeance. Hammer himself is so heedless in his own pursuit of the "Great Whatsit" that his girl has to prod him at one point with a mocking "Remember me?" And the more the characters forget the woman who has asked to be remembered and accounted for, the closer events move toward apocalypse. In curious counterpoint to the screams, which punctuate the movement towards destruction, there also sound through various scenes the voice of Caruso, and the music of *Swan Lake* and *Martha*—music that would seem, in the context of the action, to echo in a void. *Kiss Me Deadly* takes us surely to the farthest edge of the nihilistic divide.

In the ambiguities of an Aldrich film a commingling occurs, however crude or extravagant, of populist with older avant-garde moods and styles. I have earlier referred to Conrad; with *Kiss Me Deadly*, Aldrich surely brings us as close to the nihilistic abyss as the author of *Nostromo*. So, too, such Aldrich protagonists as Kirk Douglas in *The Last Sunset* or Michael Caine in *Too Late the Hero* or Burt Lancaster in *Apachee* or Beryl Reid in *The Killing of Sister George* are marked by as deep an alienation in mood and sensibility as the lead figures of a Conrad or a Camus. And of the most primitive in the Aldrich gallery of antiheroes, Mike Hammer, we may note his apparent kinship with T. S. Eliot's Apeneck Sweeney. Links of this sort with the older manner and concerns of the modernist line root Aldrich's genre pieces in cultural history and in doing so reinforce their present claim on us.

NOTE

[1] Parker Tyler, *Magic and Myth of the Movies,* 2nd ed. (New York: Simon and Schuster, 1970) 107–08.

8. HIGH PASSION AND LOW ART: FASSBINDER'S NARRATIVE STRATEGIES

Brigitte Peucker

"I LET THE AUDIENCE feel *and* think." Norbert Sparrow draws this title for his Fassbinder interview from the director's vehement assertion of a counter-Brechtian aesthetic stance:

> Q. "While your films are melodramatic, you have added the dimension of distanciating the emotions with respect to the spectator. Some critics have compared this to Brecht's *verfremdungseffect* [sic]; you reject this analogy, don't you?"

> A. "Absolutely! Intellectual thought is a process of references and categories but it shouldn't be practiced in such a quick and facile manner. With Brecht you see the emotions and you reflect upon them as you witness them, but you never feel them. That's my interpretation and I think I go farther than he did in that I let the audience *feel and think*.[1]"

Fassbinder and his critics alike have been voluble about his indebtedness to Hollywood and to the conventions of melodrama, and they have been equally insistent about the importance of the distanciation devices that interrupt his narratives.[2] But in the attempt to describe Fassbinder's techniques, it is precisely the *interplay* between melodrama and distanciation—between "low art" and "high art," the art of the masses and the art of the educated, between emotion and reason—that must remain at issue. Like Brecht, Fassbinder follows the principle that the various components of the work of art (camera movement, soundtrack, lighting, etc.) should remain distinguishable from one another so each component is thrown into relief, yet remains a part of a functioning whole: this, in part, is what Benjamin means when he speaks of interruption as a major structuring principle of Brecht's epic theater.[3] But the principle of disruption in Fassbinder occurs with respect to a narrative, a narrative which flaunts its intent to tug at the spectator's heartstrings and which acccordingly in many ways adheres to the conventions that determine popular culture—or "low art."

Together then, the elements of distanciation and melodrama constitute the dynamism of Fassbinder's films, their "dialectic principle of dynamics,"[4] to use Eisenstein's definition of the creative tension that characterizes film in general. It is my intention to point to instances in Fassbinder's films in which the tension between "reason" and "emotion" functions thematically, structurally, and at the level of recurrent images. All of these aspects of meaning are pertinent to the consideration of genre, with which my discussion will begin.

In Fassbinder's work, the expectations that ordinarily follow from melodramatic plotting are undermined by his Brechtian, self-conscious attention to the medium of film, to his "means of production." On the other hand, the deliberate opacities of formal reflexiveness, when used as an alienation effect by Fassbinder, often begin in their turn as experiments with the expectations that are generated by the most familiar and melodramatic genres. For example, *The American Soldier,* an early film, applies the logic of the gangster film to a plot that is not wholly explained by this logic, making actions seem unmotivated, events empty and self-referential. Political "lessons" interrupt the narrative and bring it into relief: the maid narrates a complete and largely unrelated story of suffering against the backdrop of a couple in bed, creating a kind of counterpoint designed to remind us of the close connection between sexual and social exploitation. Ultimately it is "love," by which in this case one can only mean unrepressed Oedipal ties and sexual bondage in general, which gradually explains the whole action—a competition between gangland powers—in the context of the Primal Scene. This emergence of a coherent pattern counteracts the initial sense of meaninglessness in the film without in the least overcoming its essential strangeness. In *The American Soldier,* Fassbinder juxtaposes the generic conventions that originate in an archetypal theater, in this case the *Oedipus,* with the conventions of the gangster film, ironically allowing "high art" (or at least its accepted interpretation) to supply the emotions which illuminate "low art."

He stages a similar interillumination in *The Bitter Tears of Petra von Kant.* In this film he appropriates the neoclassical conventions of theatrical staging. His point is that, owing to the capitalistically-induced bankruptcy of human emotions, the conventions of the classical stage (which are also, of course, Brecht's target) are suitable only as an ironic backdrop for bathos and melodrama. The classical Unity of Place becomes the prison of the womb-like bedroom; the neoclassical division of dramatic action into five acts is here reduced to the periodic changes of clothing and wigs, showing that high culture has become "haute couture." In the same vein the tragic heroine is an aristocrat like her prototypes, but her "passion," in this case for another woman, is cathartically released in an atmosphere of irony and bathos, and her fatuous reliance on bromidic proverbs for intellectual sustenance replaces the high-minded rigor and narrow distillation of classical diction. The oppressive closure of the plot is reinforced by the sense of infinite repeatability we feel at the end of the film. Its fifth act only suggests another first act to follow.

The tension between "high" and "low" art, the tension that gives so many of Fassbinder's films their particular tone, should govern the interpretation of *Lili Marleen* (whose subtitle, fittingly, is "The Story of a Song"). In fact, the failure to perceive the biting irony of this tension has misled many critics into an underestimation of the film's complexity. (One has read too often that *Lili Marleen* is "nothing but" a melodrama, and an irresponsible one at that, given the grimness of its historical setting.) The story-book, rags-to-riches love of Willi and Robert, darkened by the shadow of a disapproving father, expresses itself in a series of nearly moribund clichés on the level of narrative and dialogue—as when, for instance, Robert,

67

staunchly refusing to give Willi up, intones "I love her" to an accompaniment of operatic music.

Despite its soap-opera quality, this love affair between kitsch and art—between the entertainer, the singer of one maudlin song that enthralls the masses, and the classical pianist and conductor—is presented as the major vehicle of the film's ambivalent themes and values. Within the context of wartime history when it is baldly presented with all of its ugly determinants on display (as it is on occasion in this film), the affair of Willi is doomed to failure. Just so, one may say that Fassbinder as a filmmaker is doomed to failure when the war and the holocaust (topics which are still perhaps too immediate for the dispassion of form) are his subjects. It is for this reason, in part, that the love affair tends to displace the holocaust in constituting the film's center.

The liaison between these two themes is, of course, the identity of the two lovers—a prominent member of the Jewish underground and a German woman—and, more subtly and more easily overlooked, the ideological significance, in itself by no means simple, of their also being a "serious" artist and a "popular" artist. Robert is an upper-class representative of high culture; he plays the piano in a bar only when his love for Willi forces him to separate from his father, who is shocked that Robert should prostitute his art in "a place like this." In the end, of course, it is vanity and class allegiance that cause Robert to return to the stage to take his bows after his overwhelmingly successful concert (it is one of the melodramatic "coincidences" of the plot that Willi returns to Zürich and to him at this very moment), leaving Willi to face his wife alone. Abandoned, Willi leaves the concert hall to walk out into the night. As she approaches the water's edge, the camera is held on the film's final image of rippling waves, and the spectator may make the connection between the final moment of the narrative and the conclusion of so many nineteenth-century penny novels in which the servant girl relinquishes her life to the Seine or the Thames after her rejection by her "gentleman" lover. Fassbinder has the wisdom to leave the ending of *Lili Marleen* open, however, not so much, I think, to accommodate the "write your own ending" didacticism of Brecht in this case, but rather because the film simply couldn't bear this kind of trivialization. The audience gets the message, however; "high art" is ruthless and self-serving, even if those who practice it are politically-engaged, genuine people, with an ability to love, and even if, as is the case here, performing the particular work of art is in itself a political statement. Robert's success in conducting Mahler's Eighth Symphony seems a celebration of the end of the war and the regime that had classified Mahler among the "decadents."

Willi's art, such as it is, is more ambiguous yet. An opportunist and survivor not unlike Maria Braun, Willi first sings, as she tells Robert, "just to survive." Eventually, however, hers becomes the art of the people, the very accessibility of which makes it possible for it to be appropriated by the Nazi regime; the sentimentality that moves the soldiers on the front ultimately allows the song "Lili Marleen" to become a political instrument. Ironically, the very fact that the song consists of anti-war lyrics expressing the soldiers' fear of death— Fassbinder tells us that Goebbels called it a "Schnulze mit Totentanzgeschmack"[5]—was what obligated the Nazi regime to adopt it in order to subvert its potential subversiveness. Fassbinder makes it clear that Hitler and his henchmen "buy" Willi not just as a symbol for the Reich, but for their personal use as well. Willi has perhaps the same weakness, the same vulnerability to evil purposes, as her song. Later on, her political conversion, or perhaps enlightenment, is effected by Robert, who wins her over to the underground, but we realize that for a woman like Willi, it is essential to "risk all for the sake of the man she loves"; she is "on his side" at least in part in order to be "at his side." While the simple obliviousness to racial issues that her behavior always reflects is perhaps the best possible politics, it also shows that she will never care enough about generalization to take political issues seriously.

"History" in *Lili Marleen* is presented in two ways: it is sometimes given in its particularity, as in the nuanced representation of the specific struggles of the Jewish underground (on the level of narrative), and sometimes schematically as distanciation effect, as in the many interpolated shots of the war. These latter, highly-stylized shots, suffused with a blue light,[6] are scenes of barracks and camps and shots of killing and chaos presented in the choreographed slow motion of a dream. Fassbinder cuts to the same shots over and over again, contrasting them with the more or less verisimilar progress of his main narrative. They are an allegorical counterpoint and what they represent is their own inadequacy: that which is overwhelmingly immediate, they seem to say, can only be presented through the dense medium of melodrama. In short, as so often in Fassbinder—and as any partisan of the American soap opera will agree

—the most faithful response to high passion is low art. The war footage represents the extreme of this idea, but the longing for home and the beloved, which never ceases to be the focus of Fassbinder's attention, is more subtly melodramatized within the narrative itself.

"History" also exists in a series of radio broadcasts which observe the same dichotomy between the verisimilar and the exaggerated: sometimes they present actual events in a straightforward manner, and sometimes they are propagandistic or "fictionalized." The coming together of the particular and the general, of individualized private and representative public history, occurs for example at the train station where Willi and her pianist hear that Belgrade has just been captured: This "public" triumph is then reflected in their private triumph as they hear their recording of "Lili Marleen" for the first time. This moment also connects the tragedy of the war effort with the trivial emotion of the popular song even while it suggests that no other emotion is available. Repeatedly, shots of soldiers listening to "Lili Marleen" are juxtaposed with scenes of violence and death, and the whole is touched by an indivisible pathos.

A central issue of *Lili Marleen* is clearly the difficulty we have as individuals in distinguishing between the magnitude of public events and our own lives, which are important only to ourselves. Lest we miss this point, Fassbinder makes a parable of it in a story that is told toward the end of the film. After the war, Willi is on her way to see Robert in Switzerland, walking through the woods (the enchanted forest of the German fairytale) when an admirer tells her a story. It is not much of a story—simply this: that a pimp was said to have murdered his prostitute in this same wood. Willi shivers; she is unusually interested in this event, perhaps even improperly so, considering the fact that millions have just been murdered by an exploitative dictator. When Willi presses her companion for more information, he merely answers, "I don't know what happened, but a poet turned the story into a novel." As Willi, too, has prostituted her art to the Nazis, her interest may come from her identification with the murder victim—and now Fassbinder has turned her story into a film! As an artist, Fassbinder must identify not so much with the victim as with the poet, who turned human tragedy into art, or sensationalistic kitsch, depending on how one looks at it.

Willi's art is certainly kitsch: it is performed naively enough, but still in the hope of fame and personal profit. The sentimentality of the song moves the masses, and the audience of the film must be prepared to admit that it is moved as well, but precisely because it is so universally moving, it becomes the instrument of political exploitation. It is for this reason that Brecht tried to banish emotion from his plays, and this must then be the point of crisis in Fassbinder's knowing departure, as an artist, from the Brechtian theory. Fassbinder indicates his condemnation of Willi's song by cutting back and forth between the singing and acts of violence, between Willi throwing kisses and concentration camp scenes.

In all of this he seems to agree with Hannah Arendt's conviction that the root of such an evil as Nazism is banality. But Robert's art, on the other hand—"high art"—is cold and impersonal, and Willi in turn becomes its sacrificial victim. Fassbinder's own art, finally, which sets out to balance kitsch and formalism, melodrama and allegory, is nevertheless like the art of the poet of the parable; he uses violence and suffering to gain the acclaim of his audience. It is partly the individual whom he exploits—in yet another ambiguous scene we are left unsure whether Willi's spiritual "murder" by Robert will result in suicide—and partly the whole course of history. In using the nightmare of World War II as the subject of his film, Fassbinder must ask himself whether he too is not exploiting material that is important to him in part because it guarantees pathos.

In confronting the motives of the artist with such relentless honesty, Fassbinder is treading on dangerous ground in *Lili Marleen*. The song "Lili Marleen" remains powerfully moving for a German audience, which has never been particularly conscious that this is a "Nazi song." The question then is how the audience can be expected to react to the effect of the song; does it draw the audience in by evoking the same sentimental feelings that originally moved its public—hence potentially evoking sympathy for the motives of the war as well as for its victims—or does it distance the audience by grating on its nerves, as it must in the scene in which it is used to torture Robert? (After all, popular culture depends on repetition, the basis of brainwashing: the number of times it is played determines the place of a song in the Top 40.) Soap opera is a mesmerism induced by the recurrence of situations. Is it possible that Fassbinder would like to have it both ways? One wonders whether, in *Lili Marleen,* Fassbinder's parodistic style is not unrecognizable as parody to most spectators, and whether his central alienation effect, the song itself, does not instead run the danger of drawing us in. The song is, after all, a form of art that Fassbinder cannot help applauding, since it speaks directly to the heart.

The conjunction of reason and emotion remains an ambiguous one, then, however honestly its consequences are recognized, but in saying that it is ambiguous one also says that it forms an open-ended dialectic, and it is in that form that it dictates the structure of many of Fassbinder's films. He uses the technique of *framing* to suggest the suppression of emotion within the confines of reason, the natural effect of which is the periodic violent release of emotion from reason or of anarchy from order. *The Marriage of Maria Braun,* for instance, begins with Maria as a bride, framed by the window of a ruined building, with bombs exploding around her, and the narrative proper ends with another explosion, as the stove blows up and the house bursts into flames just as the bride is reunited with her husband. In both the beginning and the end, this frame contains within itself the volatile dynamics of union and dissolution. Similarly, the opening of *Chinese Roulette* is a static, interminable shot of a woman seated by a window in a moment of reverie, presumably listening to the operatic music on the soundtrack. In *Chinese Roulette,* the contrast of the visual tableau and the operatic music—which often represents melodramatic yearnings in Fassbinder characters — anticipates the outbreak of violence to come. The film ends with another freeze frame, this time of the castle, the setting of the emotional pyrotechnics that constitute the narrative; and as the spectator gazes at the motionless image, a shot is heard to ring out. *Mother Küsters Goes to Heaven* is framed by violence as well, though the violence is more indirectly presented. The film begins with a radio broadcast of the murder and suicide committed by Mother Küsters's husband, and ends with a report—with the written credits of the screenplay over a shot of Mother Küsters's face—of a conflict between the forces of order and the forces of anarchy during which Mother Küsters and a terrorist are killed. The balance between Brechtian reportage, the freeze frame, and the narrative of passion and violence is carefully maintained.

It should be noted that these scenes of sudden violence, these outbreaks of anarchic, Dionysian forces, are not signs of liberation, but are rather emblematic in themselves (as formal frames) of entrapment. They hem in the narrative proper. In enclosing a melodramatic yet also allegorical and didactic plot within a frame dominated by the irrational and inexplicable, Fassbinder consciously undermines the analytical aspect of his enterprise by pointing to the incomprehensibility of human motivation. It is the obscurity of the psyche that causes the obscurity that surrounds the death of Maria Braun—is it an accident?—is it a murder?—is it a suicide? There are moments and images in the film by means of which the spectator could make a case for any of the solutions just mentioned, but Fassbinder purposely does not provide us with enough "evidence" to make any one solution conclusive. Just so, as we have seen, we do not know who is shot at the end of *Chinese Roulette,* or whether Willi drowns herself at the end of *Lili Marleen.*

Again and again, these devices reinforce the oppressive closure of the narrative situation. Potentially, the circularity that they impose on the linear narrative may come to suggest that the human predicament is unresolvable. This view is tantamount, of course, to an admission of pessimism about the value of social change, and must therefore pose difficulties for even a revisionist disciple of Brecht. To evade this dilemma, Fassbinder often prevents these framing devices from becoming completely closed. The ending of *Ali: Fear Eats the Soul* is open enough to hold out encouragement. Here Fassbinder refuses the correspondence of beginning and ending: the film begins with the meeting of Ali and Emmi in a bar, but does not end with their reunion there, as it would in a melodrama of the type on which the film is in some ways based. Rather, it withholds the "happy end" of such a reunion, and concludes with another scene in which additional complications arise. The nature of contemporary German society, Fassbinder is saying, does not allow an easy resolution to the problems of this couple. Yet the film concludes with Emmi's personal resolve to change what is presented to her as a social inevitability; it is an ending, then, that at least admits the possibility of continuation through change. Just so, the dreary montage of *Bundespräsidenten* with which *Maria Braun* actually concludes is a Brechtian device which distances the spectator and once more opens the film to allegory. The ghostly chain of faces has a missing link, the omission, namely, of Willy Brandt, an absence that prompts us to remember the possibility of progress, "absent" today, but potentially as present as Brandt was present in the past.

The creative dynamic caused by the juxtaposition of reason and emotion, of Brechtian and melodramatic signification, can even be traced to the level of the image in Fassbinder. Again *The Marriage of Maria Braun* provides us with an example. In this film the cigarette is precisely the kind of multivalent image that functions within both systems of signification. It is associated with compulsion and emotional dependence, but this association is mediated for the *cinéaste*, however, by the movies of the forties and fifties which constantly use the cigarette as a prop that signifies an emotionally-heightened situation. In *Maria Braun,* this prop is used ironically by Fassbinder as a distanciation device when Hermann, returning from the war to find his wife in bed with her lover (a melodramatic moment if there ever was one), temporarily ignores the lovers and crosses the room eagerly to take a cigarette from the pack he sees lying by the window. In other words, the highly charged emotional moment is interrupted by the deliberate misappropriation of an action conventionally associated with such moments, for the film has led us to understand in earlier scenes that Hermann's overwhelming desire for a cigarette stems not from the turmoil of the moment but from his wartime deprivation of nicotine. Furthermore, cigarettes function not only within the realm of emotion and compulsion in *Maria Braun*. Given that cigarettes were literally currency in Germany during and after the war, they figure on the level of allegory as well. The beginning of Maria's Mother Courage-like foray into "trade" and business occurs when she bargains with her mother, trading two packs of cigarettes for her mother's brooch. Finally, of course, the spectator is led to believe (but denied the certainty of *knowing*) that the lighting of a cigarette causes the stove to explode and thus brings about Maria's death. This is an event which can be said to sum her up. Formerly a nonsmoker, she has now submitted to compulsions of which smoking is only one indication, and she is also shown, via the motif of the cigarette, to have bartered herself and lost the bargain.

Lili Marleen owes much to *Maria Braun*, but what is emphasized in this later film—that high passion is best conveyed by low art—is only indirectly pertinent to *Maria Braun*. In *Maria Braun* the dominant reference is not to popular, penny-novel fiction, but to the Brechtian allegory of *Mother Courage*. History takes its course, but Maria Braun, like Mother Courage, never essentially changes; she merely takes on the outward appearance of change that is reflected in her clothing and hairstyles. Maria, who prides herself on being "mutig" (courageous), also dedicates her life, like Mother Courage, to financial gain. *Her* passion—the love for her husband which she never questions and which she sees as the motive for her desire for financial security—is a cold, sublimated passion that seems to support the converse of my assumption, namely, that "low passion," intellectualized passion, finds its only adequate expression in an appeal to the intellect that is embodied in "high art." It is not surprising that critics repeatedly mention Maria Braun's allegorical character, the link between her personal history, her absorption in a materialistic dream, and German national history since the war. Fittingly, it is in the *melodramatic* moment of her death that Maria Braun escapes allegorization. Disappearing in her own right, as a human subject for whom compassion and distaste must be mingled, she gives way to the stark tableau that summarizes the era she had hitherto allegorized. This moment is one of Fassbinder's most successful confrontations between analysis and catharsis.

NOTES

[1] Norbert Sparrow, "'I Let the Audience Feel *and* Think,'— An Interview with Rainer Werner Fassbinder," *Cinéaste* 8, No. 2 (1977): 20–21.

[2] Sparrow, "Interview," 20–22; Thomas Elsaesser, "A Cinema of Vicious Circles," in *Fassbinder,* ed. Tony Rayns (London: BFI, 1976) 24–36; R.W. Fassbinder, "Fassbinder on Sirk," trans. Thomas Elsaesser, *Film Comment* 11, No. 6, (Nov.–Dec. 1975): 22–24; James C. Franklin, "The Films of Fassbinder: Form and Formula," *Quarterly Review of Film Studies* 5, No. 2 (Spring 1980): 169–82.

[3] Walter Benjamin, "What is Epic Theater?," in *Illuminations,* ed. Hannah Arendt (New York: Schocken Books, 1973) 151.

[4] Sergei Eisenstein, "A Dialectical Approach to Film Form," in *Marxism and Art: Writings in Aesthetics and Criticism,* ed. Berel Lang and Forrest Williams (New York: Longman, 1972) 358.

[5] Roughly translated: "soupy love song with a *danse macabre* atmosphere."

[6] This "blue light" strongly recalls the Leni Riefenstahl film of that title *(The Blue Light,* 1932). In fact, there are many parallels to be drawn between Willi and the film goddess of the Nazi regime.

9. REFORMATION AND ITS COUNTERFEIT: THE RECOVERY OF MEANING IN *HENRY IV, PART ONE*

F. Nick Clary

AFTER A LITTLE tavern "play" designed to prepare Hal for a meeting with his father at court, Falstaff advises the Prince: "never call a true piece of gold a counterfeit." One editor prints, "thou art essentially mad, without seeming so," as Falstaff's next line. However, he glosses "essentially made" in his note for the line in question.[1] The Variorum editors list over three dozen entries which elaborate the controversy over this passage. Although the edition quoted above does not mention this controversy, the combination of the line and its gloss could provoke a similar confusion among readers unfamiliar with the available scholarship. The edition to which I have referred bears the label "An Authorized Text" on the title page; however, the paperback cover advertises "An Authoritative Text." I am not sure which label the editor would approve, and I hesitate to guess whether the author would consider this "revised" version of his play "a true piece of gold" or "a counterfeit."

From the earliest commentaries to the most recent critical studies, Shakespeare's Prince Hal has been the subject of persistent and varied controversy.[2] Literary scholars, however, have not so much created the controversy as revealed its inevitability; if the playwright has not written an intentionaly ambiguous work, he has at least constructed a text that reveals the difficulties of interpretation. From the moment that Hal is first mentioned near the end of *Richard II* (V, iii), his words and actions are the objects of onstage commentary from every quarter.[3] The experience of Shakespeare's plays about Prince Hal approximates, in some respects, the reading of several source accounts concerning the exploits of Henry Monmouth.

Among the broad range of pre-Shakespearian sources, there is considerable variation. Whether the source is historical or nonhistorical in its methods, moral or political in its ideals, each interpretation is an effect of a particular appropriation of Prince Hal as a model and a testament to specific beliefs about the causes that shape events and the forces that govern the transformations in human character and behavior.[4] Conflicts of interpretation, which are the legacy of diversified source records, may have been a central concern of Shakespeare in his second historical tetralogy. Problems of interpretation will be my concern in this present reading of *Henry IV, Part One.*

In Shakespeare's earliest reference to Hal *(Richard II,* V, iii), the newly crowned King expresses concern about the political effect of his son's "madcap" behavior.[5] Although he has not seen the Prince for three months, Henry has heard rumors that Hal has been haunting the taverns of London. When he urges the nobles gathered at Windsor Castle to find out what they can about his son, his anxiety is clear: "If any plague hang over us, 'tis he." Hotspur is quick to report that he has seen Hal and told him of the jousting matches to be held at Oxford. Hal's answer, that he would go the "stews, / And from the common'st creature pluck a glove" to wear as a "favor" (V, iii, 16–19), would seem to confirm the King's suspicions. Yet Henry reads in this reply "some sparks of better hope, which elder years / May happily bring forth" (V, iii, 21–22).

Later, in the first scene of *Henry IV, Part One,* the King once again laments the "riot and dishonor" which "stain the brow" of his son. Between Henry's two references to Hal, no change has been reported in the Prince's behavior. The King's reading of his son, however, has grown less optimistic, for his hope now lies in the improbable fancy that fairies might have exchanged his Harry for Percy's when they were infants (I, i, 86–90). While offstage audiences may speculate about the meaning of Hal's behavior, Henry's reading of it as sometimes dangerously irresponsible and sometimes harmlessly immature indicates that the Prince's conduct can generate variant effects of meaning at different times and under different circumstances.[6]

When Shakespeare's Prince makes his first appearance in *Henry IV, Part One* (I, ii), his behavior in conversation is note-worthy in its strategy. Falstaff speaks first: "Now, Hal, what time of day is it, lad?" Hearing the question, Hal says that Falstaff cannot mean what his words signify. In light of what he believes about this speaker and of what he takes to be the situation, Hal claims, "thou hast forgotten to demand that truly which thou wouldst truly know." Initially Falstaff's inquiry about the time is taken to be an effect of forgetfulness induced by the speaker's idleness of life. Hal goes on to insist that the only way he can comprehend Falstaff is to assume that a system of substitutions is in play which invests the question with its apparent identity:

> Unless hours were cups of sack and minutes capons
> and clocks the tongues of bawds and dials the signs
> of leaping-houses and the blessed sun himself a fair
> hot wench in flame-coloured taffeta, I see no reason
> why thou shouldst be so superfluous to demand the
> time of the day. (I, ii, 6–13).[7]

This first exchange is instructive, for Hal's reading of Falstaff illus-trates how assumptions about a speaker and situation may be opera-tive in the process of understanding. By extension, whether the in-terpreter is a father or a fat companion, an historian or a contributor to folklore, a literary scholar or an unsophisticated reader,[8] there will always be some interplay between perceptible data and the network of beliefs and habits that shape the interpretation of Hal's own words and actions.

As the scene in question continues, Hal baffles Falstaff at every turn and dismantles each of his attempted readings of the con-versation in progress. Hal's evasions and indirections frustrate each of Falstaff's efforts to find familiar ground on which to stand. Failing to assure himself of the meaning of Hal's speech, the "old lad of the castle" finds himself in a verbal wilderness without a map, and he complains self-consciously about his condition (call it mel-ancholy, vanity, or what he will). Falstaff, however, may not be the only one affected this way by Shakespeare's Prince. For example, those who might have expected that their direct experience of Hal would guarantee a clear and certain reading of his character and conduct might have found instead that the presence of the Prince has only served to dispel the hope that contact with him could be free of the subjectiveness that colors rumors and reports. In this scene Hal is exasperating, for he does not stand still long enough to be a stable object of attention. Whenever he seems to vanish behind clouds of verbal wit, offstage interpreters are left to consider their own operations in startlingly self-conscious ways. If they should ask themselves what they are doing, they might find that Falstaff is not the only one baffled by Hal.

Near the end of this scene, Poins enters to propose a robbery of pilgrims and traders outside London, and Falstaff is anxious to ask Hal to join in. The Prince replies, "Who, I rob? I a thief? not I, by my faith." When Falstaff accuses him of lacking "honesty" for refusing to be a robber, Hal adjusts his speech to the terms of the persuasion. If robbing is princely behavior in Falstaff's system, then Hal's refusal to be a thief must be accommodated. He responds, "Well then, once in my days I'll be a madcap." When Falstaff commends Hal, "Why, that's well said," the Prince clarifies his decision by insisting that, in light of the current exchange, madcap behavior can only mean staying at home and not participating in the robbery.

Before Hal is left alone on the stage, however, Poins urges him to join in a scheme to rob Falstaff and his confederates at Gadshill, insisting that the "virtue of this jest" will be in the "reproof" of Falstaff's lies afterwards. When Hal agrees, his "dissolute" conduct can be read as part of a program to reprove dishonesties. But whatever Hal's conversations with Falstaff and Poins might seem to illustrate, the meaning of his appearance so far in this scene cannot be understood as obvious or self-evident; it must be interpreted.

When Poins bids farewell and exits, Hal is left alone onstage. For the first time, Shakespeare's Prince speaks without the conditioning restraints of an onstage audience. In the conventional privacy of soliloquy, he claims to know precisely what he is doing. When Hal credits himself with success in creating his own reputation for "loose" behavior, he momentarily unsettles the available readings of his conduct. Whether the Prince's behavior has been consistently or variously read as dangerously irresponsible or harmlessly immature or indirectly reproving, it had never before been openly considered as part of a calculated political strategy. In this new light, his scheme looks like a Machiavellian gloss on the parable of the prodigal son. Although editorial notes may guide readers to interpret this speech in a particular way, and critical commentaries often encourage a specific assumption about the author's intention, when Hal anticipates the moment when he will throw off his "loose" behavior in a dazzle of "glitt'ring" reformation, he creates the possibility of conflicting interpretations at every turn.[9]

One important question that Hal's soliloquy raises is this: how can one recognize reformation when one sees it? In light of his speech, there are several ways to read the action that follows in the play. Insofar as a speaker's description of himself defines and determines the meaning of the actions he performs, it is possible to understand Hal as an essentially consistent character.[10] According to this reading, Hal may be said to remain committed to his plan of manipulating public opinion by engineering a moment when the illusion of "loose behavior" will give way to the impression of "glitt'ring" reform. No more virtuous than his father and no less calculating than Richard III, Hal's success would be a tribute to Machiavelli.[11] On the other hand, it is possible to understand Hal as a character who subsequently undergoes a remarkable transformation in a moment of actual conversion. This latter reading would find miracle, in place of manipulation, in Hal's story and dramatic irony, rather than political program, in his soliloquy. In this light, Prince Hal becomes the real convert that he had claimed he would only play.[12] Both of these readings depend on the fixing of reformation in a single event. Whether played or actual, the casting off of dissolute behavior is "foreshadowed" as a moment of conversion which will be publicly recognized and generally welcomed. In order to be effective, Hal's reformation cannot be suspected of counterfeit; it must be indistinguishable from the real thing.[13]

The problem of distinguishing between reformation and its counterfeit, however, is not limited to one unrepeated occasion; it is a persistent condition of interpretation. In the tavern, at the palace, and on the battlefield, Hal enacts confessions of his misconduct and promises to reform. Onstage interpreters, whose experiences with the Prince are more restricted than those of offstage audiences, find themselves challenged to take the Prince at his word. For example, when the tavern play ends, in which Falstaff and Hal had alternately assumed the roles of King and Prince, Falstaff delivers a mock ultimatum: "banish plump Jack, and banish all the world." Hal makes a cryptic reply: "I do, I will." No one onstage seems to take the Prince at his word, for he is assumed to be merely playing.[14] Offstage interpreters, however, might recognize this scene as Hal's moment of mysterious conversion from a life of wayward prodigality. As such, it does not appear to be politically motivated, and it lacks the impact that his "reformation" was designed to have. Nonetheless, it is possible to read a firm purpose of amendment in his reply to Falstaff.[15] Although several critics and commentators have found this scene to be more purposeful than the comic diversion it is taken to be onstage, many consider Hal's closing remark to be either evidence of callousness in the speaker or irony in the playwright rather than reformation in the prince.[16] In most of the scenes after Hal's soliloquy, offstage audiences have discovered meanings in actions and words which go virtually unnoticed by those onstage.[17] Furthermore, offstage interpreters have regularly found themselves in considerable disagreement despite the advantage of seeing the events from a perspective which is not limited by onstage involvement in the action or biased by political allegiance.[18]

Later, under the pressure of his father's badgering speculations at the palace (III, ii), Hal has several opportunities to explain himself. Whatever designs the King might have in suggesting that his son's "vile participation" could be God's punishment for his own "misreadings," he is surely not confessing his guilt.[19] When Hal is asked to explain his madcap conduct, he admits to "some things true," which he excuses as the "wanderings" of youth, and dismisses other charges as the "tales" of "pick-thanks and newsmongers."[20] Still, he asks pardon in the name of "true submission." Despite Henry's exclamation,"God pardon thee!," this king sees no place for morality within the political arena; when he presses on to lecture Hal on good conduct, he stresses effectiveness, rather than ethics. Describing his own political shrewdness and mocking Richard's ineptitude, Henry details his success in supplanting the annointed King. The time might seem opportune for Hal to reveal the politic method in his madness and to predict success for himself based on the simple logic of his soliloquy.[21] He promises instead, "I shall hereafter . . . be more myself." By now both speakers may be engaged in the kind of doublethink that Worcester had earlier described: "The king will always think him in our debt, / And think we think ourselves unsatisfied" (I, iii, 283–284). Offstage audiences are left to infer the meanings taken by both of the onstage hearers which provide the contexts for interpreting the meanings of their replies. Not only is reference to some "subtext" required, but citations from "the text itself" are insufficient as evidence of meaning unless they are persuasively interpreted.[22] Onstage, however, Hal's apparent promise to reform leads directly to the King's denunciation of him as his "nearest and dearest enemy" who might fight against him "under Percy's pay."[23] To this, the Prince replies, "Do not think so; you shall not find it so,"[24] and he goes on to prophesy "some glorious day" when he will exchange his own indignities for Hotspur's "glorious deeds." When Hal promises to fight to the death for his father against the rebels and seals his pledge with a vow, the King exults.[25]

Whether the offstage audience is expected to forget Hal's soliloquy or Hal effectually forgets it himself, when his vow reintroduces God to the field of the conversation, it could signal a diminishment of his belief in the efficacy of political strategy.[26] At any rate, as the generalities of his soliloquy are displaced by the particulars of developing events, Hal's willingness to concede errors in his ways may be growing into a recognition of the essential error in his thinking. At this point in the play, offstage interpreters may notice in Hal's behavior a gradual recovery of the meaning of reformation as a process, which depends for its achievement on the progressive unlearning of what he had seemed to know already. The idea that education is the proper process description for the Prince's reformation may have occurred to several offstage interpreters even before Warwick's claim in *Henry IV, Part Two,* and the conclusion drawn by the Archbishop of Canterbury and the Bishop of Ely in *Henry V.* [27] The difference that I am suggesting here is that Hal's transformation is a counterprogressive process; it is not so much a gaining of knowledge through varied experiences as a losing of what he seemed to know in favor of more ancient wisdoms. The notion that Hal could have known already what he seems to be learning could be a way of glossing Vernon's later description of him to Hotspur: it was "As if he mastered there a double spirit / Of teaching and of learning instantly" (V, ii, 63–64). In this light, Hal's transformation from a politically cynical strategist to an idealistic defender of the King is directly related to his repeated enactment of a promise to reform his life while confessing the looseness of his ways.

On the eve of the battle at Shrewsbury, Worcester and Vernon represent the rebels in a meeting at the King's camp (V, i). After Worcester and the King exchange accusations which trumpet their suspicions and distrust,[28] Hal steps forward to praise Hotspur for his celebrated "deeds" and to confess his own shame for having been a "truant to chivalry."[29] Furthermore, he offers to "try fortune" in a single fight with Hotspur, in order "to save the blood on either side" (V, i, 83–100). Whether offstage audiences read Hal in good faith (as gold) or with suspicion (as counterfeit), the King, for whatever reason, sets his son's proposal aside and offers his "grace" to the rebels if they will yield to him.[30]

When the meeting ends and the rebels leave, each negotiator for an alternative to open battle reveals his doubts and his suspicions of the others. Worcester, for example, expresses his fear of "suppositions" everywhere and his certainty that "interpretation" will always "misquote" his looks. In this, he reveals another problem which arises when one attempts to read others: the hazard of being read. The failure of peaceful reconciliation here may be one of the inevitable consequences of private interpretation in an age of pervasive self-interest and profound disbelief.

In the final scenes of the play, while the rebel leaders are maddened by the King's men who march to their deaths "furnish'd like the king himself" (V, iii, 20), Hal relentlessly pursues Hotspur amid a flurry of reports that Percy has already been killed or captured.[31] Whatever doubts he might have about fulfilling his vow to "redeem" himself "on Percy's head" (III, ii, 132), when Hal rescues his father from Douglas, he declares that he "never promiseth but he means to pay" (V, iv, 42). As this echo from a line in his early soliloquy combines with Henry's announcement that his son has "redeemed" his "lost opinion" by driving Douglas off, Hal's politic plan and his filial pledge seem to coincide for an instant.

But the Prince does not declare his success on either count; rather he protests his father's continued suspicions and indirectly confesses his own failure to control the readings given to his words and actions: "O God! they did me too much injury / That ever said I heark'ned for your death" (V, iv, 51–52).[32] Until the end of the play, as Hal's words repeatedly recall earlier scenes and other contexts, the challenge to decide who Hal is and what he is doing is unavoidable.[33] While the characters onstage reveal the difficulties involved in reading others and in being read themselves, offstage audiences may feel pressured to hazard a belief which will provide a stable ground for reading Hal's story.

From the moment he encounters Hotspur until he gives Prince John the honor of setting Douglas free, Shakespeare's Hal challenges his interpreters' beliefs. When he meets Hotspur in the field, Hal echoes his promise to the King, though presumption rather than prophecy sounds through his claim: "think not, Percy, / To share with me in glory any more. . . .all the budding honours on thy crest / I'll crop, to make a garland for my head" (V, iv, 62–73). When he mortally wounds Hotspur, completing his rival's final estimate of himself ("thou art dust, / And food for — / For worms, brave Percy" [V, iv, 85–86]), Hal might refresh the audience's memory of his soliloquy's cocky arrogance. But in the presumed privacy of his triumph, Hal goes on to eulogize the "great heart" fallen before him and to speak again of "ill-weaved ambition" and the ironies of human mortality, but this time with moral prudence.

This is no mere repetition; it illustrates how the effects of meaning can deepen and improve as they are reiterated.[34] When Hal bends to cover Hotspur's face with his own "favours," the image that he strikes refreshes a memory of noble chivalry and restores prophetic dignity to Hal's vision of the "glorious day" of his redemption (III, ii, 132–137). However questionable his integrity and motives might be later when he promises to give Falstaff credit for killing Hotspur and when he grants Prince John the honor of disposing of Douglas, Hal's final words over the body of his fallen rival seem genuinely magnanimous:

> Adieu, and take thy praise with thee to heaven!
> Thy ignominy sleep with thee in the grave,
> But not rememb'red in thy epitaph!
> (V, iv, 99–101)

As the play ends amid a swirl of promises and poses, offstage interpreters might experience momentary trials of belief involving Hal's conditions of mind, heart, and soul. In fact, the problems of distinguishing between counterfeit and the real thing, which persist to the last lines of this play, continue through the two plays which complete the story of Hal's succession to the throne.[35] There will be many more times when interpreters will find their subject involved in unexpected actions and uttering words which test their faith in the rightness of their "settled" readings.

Because it is possible for moral choice to coincide with political necessity, idealistic motives are sometimes inextricable from utilitarian ones.[36] In the shadow of pervasive ambiguity, the reading given to Hal at any point will be conditioned by the interpreter's assumptions about man's nature and the mysteries of human experience. In times of self-doubt, pretense, and suspicion, the belief that anyone can achieve nobility in his conduct might be a necessity. During the Elizabethan Age, when the amorality of Machiavellian politics was practiced as much as it was criticized, a belief in Hal's moral recovery may, in fact, be a testimony to the possibility of regaining an ideal which had been lost.[37] If counterfeit reformation was one of the effects of challenged authority and the failure of personal conscience, it might be said that Hal gives new currency to the "real" thing near the end of *Henry IV, Part One*. If so, then this play could be a clue to Shakespeare's sense of the value of historical thinking and an invitation to faith in the possibility of "redeeming time."

NOTES

[1] Unless otherwise stated, I refer to the Sanderson edition in citations to *1 Henry IV*, ed. James L. Sanderson (New York: W.W. Norton and Company, 1969).

[2] In addition to the commentaries and studies cited in the glosses, the *Variorum Edition of Henry the Fourth, Part I* (Philadelphia: J. B. Lippincott and Company, 1936) and the *Supplement* (published in 1956 by the Shakespeare Association of America) include Appendices which sketch the major lines of the controversy. See especially *Variorum* 341–55 and 457–66; and *Supplement* 56–78 and 90–94. Recent articles and books indicate that the critical controversy is not likely to subside. I encourage my readers to attend to the documentation and consider its implications relative to the rules of evidence and persuasion.

[3] In addition to the characters in *1 Henry IV*, there are several others in *2 Henry IV* and in *Henry V* (including clerics, nobles, and the soldiery) who take various positions on the meaning of Hal's words and behavior. In these latter plays, characters are not the only commentators onstage: there is a Prologue (presented by Rumor)

and an Epilogue (spoken by a Dancer, according to one recent edition) in *2 Henry IV;* in *Henry V* there are choral introductions to each act in addition to the Prologue and Epilogue.

[4] In their interpretations of the meaning of events, these writers reveal the anomalies that derive from attributing causes sometimes to the exercises of human will and sometimes to the workings of Divine Providence. Ornstein notes that ambivalences exist not only between but within various accounts: "In Hall's as in other sixteenth-century Chronicles, moralistic judgements stand side by side with shrewdly realistic observations of political life. Next to pious exclamations and simplistic moral portraits are clear-eyed statements of the Machiavellian facts of political struggle and intrigue." See Robert Ornstein, *A Kingdom for a Stage* (Cambridge, Mass.: Harvard University Press, 1972) 20–21.

[5] For a fertile introduction to the problems of sorting out facts from legend, see Croft's expanded footnote on Elyot's reference to the Lord Chief Justice incident (Henry Stephen Croft, *The Boke Named the Governour devised by Sir Thomas Elyot,* vol. 2 [London: K. Paul, Trench and Company, 1883] fn. 6, 61–71). Willey notes: "It may be that all thought is conditioned, and so 'unfree'; even so-called 'liberal' or 'objective' thinking is directed by presuppositions, however latent or unconscious they may be. We cannot help interpreting the world from where we stand, and with a view to some hoped for destination (Basil Willey, *The English Moralists* [New York: Doubleday Company, Inc., 1964, rpt. 1967] 82).

[6] The wording here has been intentionally groomed after Abrams's rendering of the deconstructive claims of Jacques Derrida (M. H. Abrams, *A Glossary of Literary Terms,* 4th ed. [New York: Holt, Rinehart and Winston, 1981]).

[7] See "Deconstruction" in Abrams for suggestions about the implications made available by the wording of this description of Hal's procedure in "reading" Falstaff.

[8] The distinction between "literary scholar" and "unsophisticated reader" is made in light of the First Folio's opening range of readers, from "the most able" to "him that can but spell" (A3). See discussions of "literary competence" in Jonathan Culler, *Structuralist Poetics* (Ithaca, N.Y.: Cornell University Press, 1975) 113–30, and of "informed" readership in Stanley Fish, *Is There A Text In This Class?* (Cambridge, Mass.: Harvard University Press, 1980) 303–71.

[9]As a dramatic device, the soliloquy is a versatile convention. Abrams notes: "the playwright uses this device as a convenient way to convey directly to the audience information about a character's motives, intentions, and state of mind, as well as for purposes of general exposition" (180). This versatility, however, introduces ambiguity: for instance, "intention" and "state of mind" may be proper labels for the remarkably different soliloquies spoken by Richard III (*Richard III*, I, i) and by Richard II (*Richard II*, V, v), respectively. In terms of Hal's speech, the difference between political rationale (an "intention") and psychological rationalization (a "state of mind") does not appear to be a quibble. See also the commentary on "various modes of solo speech" in Daniel Seltzer, "Prince Hal and Tragic Style," *Shakespeare Survey* 30 (1977) 17–25, and notes on alternate ways that an actor might "play" this speech as well as the gloss on "variable effectiveness of the soliloquy . . . illustrated from accounts of performances" in *Shakespeare in Performance: An Introduction through Six Major Plays*, ed. John Russell Brown (New York: Harcourt Brace Jovanovich, Inc., 1976) 125–26. On the point of authorial intention, Empson notes: "Of course to decide on an author's purpose, conscious or unconscious, is very difficult. Good writing is not done unless it works for readers with opinions different from the author's." Yet Empson insists later in his book: "The crucial first soliloquy of Prince Henry was put in to save his reputation with the audience; it is a willful destruction of his claims to generosity, indeed to honesty, if only in Falstaff's sense: but this is not to say that it was a mere job with no feeling behind it. . . it cannot have been written without bitterness against the prince. . . .In having some sort of double attitude to the prince, Shakespeare was merely doing his work as a history writer" (William Empson, *Some Versions of Pastoral* [New York: New Directions Publishing Co., 1930, rpt. 1968] 3–5 and 102–05).

[10] The wording here has intentionally followed Rorty, who goes on to note that a speaker's description "may perfectly well be set aside" (Richard Rorty, *Philosophy and the Mirror of Nature* [Princeton: Princeton University Press, 1979] 349). In light of Worcester's complaints about the unalterability of the King's fixed reading of him (II, i, 282–85 and V, ii, 12–15), Hal's politic strategy might seem naive. The outcome of events in the play, however, could be introduced in support of both the optimism of Hal and the

pessimism of Worcester, though they are mutually exclusive in their assumptions.

[11] Although Tudor historians indicate that Hal's contemporaries, including his father, suspected him of political plotting long befor the events of this play, Swinburne (who likened Hal to Louis XI and Caesar Borgia) was one of the earliest proponents of this reading, but it did not become popular until after Bradley, Yeats, and G. B. Shaw argued for it (see *Variorum* 461–63). By now it has become one of the recognized interpretations of Prince Hal/Henry V. See the commentary by Fredson Bowers, "Shakespeare's Art: The Point of View," in *Literary Views,* ed. Carroll Camden (Chicago: University of Chicago Press, 1964) 45–58, which is reprinted in Sanderson, esp. 313–16. Weiss has more recently turned the corner on this reading by commending rather than blaming Hal for his policy; he labels him "the ablest 'actor'" and a "royal counterfeit" who is well suited to a "topsy-turvy, bad time" (Theodore Weiss, *The Breath of Clowns and Kings* [New York: Atheneum, 1974] 277). On this latter note, Mosse's assertion that "pious frauds" and "holy deceits" may imply "sincere attempts to meet the challenge of 'policy' and reason of state," rather than "mere hypocrisy," might shed more favorable light on Hal's reformation ploy (George L. Mosse, *The Holy Pretense* [New York: Howard Fertig, 1957, rpt. 1968] 5).

[12] In general, Tudor historians attempt to diminish the extent and/or intensity of Hal's dissoluteness by speaking of slanders and false rumors. Several, however, favor this reading, and there is considerable agreement among them about naming the time of Hal's "miraculous conversion" as the day of his coronation; see J. Dover Wilson's discussion of Fabyan's *Chronicle* of 1516 in *The Fortunes of Falstaff* (New York: Cambridge University Press, 1944) 15–35, which is reprinted in Sanderson, esp. 261–66. It might be well to mention that in *Henry V,* the Archbishop of Canterbury and the Bishop of Ely consider this interpretation but reject it, "for miracles are ceased" (I, i, 67). Brown glosses this passage: "protestants believed miracles ceased to occur after the revelation of Christ" *(William Shakespeare: The Life of Henry V,* ed. John Russell Brown [New York: The New American Library, 1965] 45). Modern historians tend to lament the lack of documentary evidence for Hal's dissolute conduct and to dismiss the possibility of miraculous conversion as a matter of superstition.

[13] Rabkin's discussion of the notion of "complementarity" might be valuable reading for those who recognize a problem here and see no convincing way to avoid what looks like an either/or choice at the crossroads of interpretation (Norman Rabkin, *Shakespeare and the Common Understanding* [New York: The Free Press, 1967] 1–29). In addition, I would like to recommend Stanley Fish, *Self-Consuming Artifacts* (Berkeley: University of California Press, 1972) 1–43 and Harold Bloom, "The Breaking of Form," *Deconstruction and Criticism* (New York: The Seabury Press, 1979) 1–22. After reading these, it might be possible to avoid lamenting the road(s) not taken.

[14] It might be argued that the Sheriff's knocking prevents any direct onstage response. It is curious, nonetheless, that while this knocking can effectively prevent interpretive responses onstage, it might be taken to be a specialized dramatic signal by interpreters offstage. See Goddard's discussion of "knocking" as a device used by Shakespeare "to betoken at a fateful moment the knocking of the inner mentor" (Harold Goddard, *The Meaning of Shakespeare,* vol. 2 [Chicago: University of Chicago Press, 1951] 207–09).

[15] Toliver, for example, calls it "a kind of official proclamation . . . a present impulse to reject comic ritual and to seek some other adjustment" (Harold O. Toliver, "Falstaff, the Prince, and the History Play," *Shakespeare Quarterly* 16 [Winter 1965]: 63–80, reprinted in Sanderson, esp. 176–79). Furthermore, Dessen notes: "Shakespeare makes it clear that the prince's summary comment ('I do, I will') is based upon accurate knowledge of his companions (emphasized again through the papers from Falstaff's pockets), complete control of himself (in evidence since I, ii), and total awareness of the debt that remains to be paid, the role that must be assumed, and the world that must eventually be banished. Hal's four revealing words are in themselves enough to explain his ultimate victory over Hotspur if only in the vision that allows him to see the future in the present (as in his soliloquy) and steer his own independent course through uncharted political and moral waters" (Alan C. Dessen, "The Intemperate Knight and the Politic Prince: Late Morality Structure in *1 Henry IV,*" *Shakespeare Studies* 7 [1974]: 159). See also Richard L. McGuire, "The Play-within-the-Play in *1 Henry IV,*" *Shakespeare Quarterly* 18 (Winter 1967): 50.

[16] Traversi finds Hal's reply "true to the Prince's character and to the tragedy of his family": he will "banish everything that cannot

be reduced to an instrument of policy in the quest for empty success" (D. A. Traversi, *"Henry IV, Part I:* History and the Artist's Vision,"* a revised reprint of his essay in *Scrutiny* [1947], in Sanderson, 322). On the other hand, Arthur C. Sprague sees "plenty of irony" in Hal's reply, though it was unavailable to audiences until the composition and presentation of *2 Henry IV,* and George L. Kittredge is careful to rule out an intention in the Prince to banish Falstaff, "for when this happens, he has 'turned from his former self'" (Variorum *Supplement,* 25–26). See also Seltzer's remarks on Hal's reply ("Prince Hal and Tragic Style" [26]).

¹⁷ Sometimes onstage interpreters find themselves at a loss to understand Hal and must ask him for an explanation. For example, earlier in this same scene, Poins plays along with Hal in the baiting of Francis. Afterwards, however, Poins turns to Hal and says, "But hark ye; what cunning match have you made with this jest of the drawer? come, what's the issue" (II, iv, 100–02). Dessen finds no such difficulty offstage: "To the audience, Prince Hal is the obvious puppetmaster who can control Francis's reactions because of his knowledge of what makes the puppet work, whereas no one else understands the purpose of the test case" (158).

¹⁸ With respect to the baiting of Francis (alluded to above), Ornstein describes the controversy it has spawned and notes one possible consequence of claims based on an assumption about Elizabethan conventions: "If Tillyard is correct the Francis episode is not a fascinating revelation of Hal's personality; it is an irrelevant and purposeless bit of low humor, which exposes Shakespeare's 'Elizabethan' snobbery and coarseness" (see Ornstein's discussion of this scene and of "Elizabethan 'thought,'" 8–11).

¹⁹ Setting aside his own earlier readings of Hal (as dangerously irresponsible or harmlessly immature), the King now finds the reproving hand of God in Hal's dissoluteness. If Hal could be thought of as a conscious scourge of God, then his designs on the King might be inferred to be similar to the indirect reproval claimed as a possible explanation of his earlier agreement to rob Falstaff at Gadshill. Ornstein, however, considers Henry's first words "a scathing rebuke," though he notes an ambivalence in the King's lecturing of Hal: "Does Henry mistake his son? Or does he know precisely how to test Hal's mettle and how to expose the princely self behind the cloak of loose behavior?" (142–43).

²⁰ Hal does not enumerate or distinguish the "tales" from the

"true things." The King and the offstage interpreters are left to assume that they know what he means.

[21] Though the phrase "method in his madness" may seem inexcusably trite, it is meant to recall the lines mentioned in the opening paragraph of this paper ("essentially mad/made"), and the commonplace that is popular in discussions of Hamlet's dealings with Claudius. See G. R. Hibbard, *"Henry IV* and *Hamlet," Shakespeare Survey* 30 (1977): 1–12.

[22] Seltzer, on the issue of Hal's subtext in this play, notes: "The words of the text, in the mode of playwriting, themselves become referential; they demand for their full effectiveness an understanding of, or at least our assumption that the character possesses, an interior life which is developing its own energies, subtextually" (26). See also persuasions in Fish regarding ambiguity and indirect speech act (268–92) and to relativism and solipsism (317–21).

[23] Ornstein cites C.L. Kingsford's introduction to *The First Life of King Henry the Fifth* (Oxford: Clarendon Press, 1911) xxi, in support of his own suggestion: "We rejoice in the thought that the greatest monarch had misspent his youth, and much prefer this fictional prince to the real one, who apparently schemed with his allies to wrest the throne from his ailing father. We would rather believe that Hal boxed the ear of Authority than that he lusted for the crown" (140).

[24] Although these two statements may be taken as distinct declarations with respect to the King's claims (a denial of the charge that he is his father's enemy and an assurance that he will never take arms with the rebels against the King), it is possible to perceive conditional logic between them (If you do not believe that I am your enemy, then you will not find that I am your enemy).

[25] In light of Hal's vow (if he "break the smallest parcel," may he "die a hundred thousand deaths"), the King's triumphant reply, "A hundred thousand rebels die in this," may be as richly ambiguous as Hal's "I do, I will."

[26] Hal's invocation of God may be an unexpected effect of Henry's political hectoring or of his own repeated enactment of a resolution to change his ways. See C. S. Lewis, *Mere Christianity* (New York: Macmillan Co., 1943, rpt. 1960) 147; and Henri Bergson, *Matter and Memory* (New York: Macmillan Co., 1959) 102. Furthermore, his vow is not a denial of Henry's charge that his son is in Richard's line (III, ii, 85–87); rather it recalls a time when the

God of Justice was believed to be the director of human events, a time like that invoked for a moment by Richard II when Mowbray and Bolingbroke were set on proving each other false (*Richard II*, I, i, and iii). In this connection, perhaps Mazzeo's analysis of Machiavelli's theory of reform might reveal a surprising irony: Machiavelli "blends two views of history—the cyclical and the regenerative. . . . Any hope of reform lies, analogically, in a retrograde movement to the more vigorous starting point. For example, any state that wishes to renew itself must return to its old ethos, a return which, Machiavelli says, can only be the work of one powerful man" (Joseph Mazzeo, *Renaissance and Revolution* [New York: Random House, 1965, rpt. 1967] 88. Ornstein, on the other hand, considers Hal's reply "a furious and boasting pledge" (142).

[27] For a survey of some recent proposals concerning the implications of Hal's education, see especially Paul A. Jorgensen, "'Redeeming Time' in Shakespeare's *Henry IV*," *Tennessee Studies in Literature* 5 (1960): 101–09; Hugh Dickson, "The Reformation of Prince Hal," *Shakespeare Quarterly* 12 (1961): 33–46; Joan Webber, "The Renewal of the King's Symbolic Role: From *Richard II* to *Henry V*," reprinted from *Texas Studies in Language and Literature* (1963) in James L. Calderwood and Harold E. Toliver, *Essays in Shakespeare* (Englewood Cliffs, New Jersey: Prentice Hall, Inc., 1970) 193–201; and Charles Mitchell, "The Education of the True Prince," *Tennessee Studies in Literature* 12 (1967): 13–21.

[28] Worcester accuses the King of a "violation" of faith which drove the rebels "for safety sake to fly," while Henry charges that "insurrection" is always able to find "water colors to impaint his cause."

[29] This Hal appears to be remarkably different from the gallant who had responded so cavalierly to Hotspur's announcement of the "triumphs at Oxford" (*Richard II,* V, iii, 16–19) and from the tavern cynic who had mocked Hotspur's braveries after his own "heroics" at Gadshill (*1 Henry IV,* II, iv, 92–101). In addition, offstage interpreters might have various expectations based on their "readings" of the scenes that have taken place in the meantime. For example, between the scene at the Palace and the eve of the battle at Shrewsbury, Hal has returned to the tavern one more time. If there is a change in him, it is that he is less amused at Falstaff's shameless refusal to own up to his extravagant indulgences and debts. For his part, Hal admits to going through Falstaff's pockets and to paying

back the robbery money after Gadshill, explaining, "I am good friends with my father and may do any thing" (III, iii, 161). Although Falstaff and Bardolph recognize this statement as a claim to be above the law and immediately propose another robbery, Hal abruptly changes the subject: "I have procured thee, Jack, a charge of foot." In a later scene, Vernon has announced to the rebel camp the approach of the King's army. His description of Hal mounting his horse (rising "like Mercury" from the ground and vaulting into his seat "As if an angel dropp'd down from the clouds" [IV, i, 106–08]) overturns Hotspur's more cynical request for news of "the nimble-footed madcap Prince of Wales," and evokes an image of "glitt'ring" reform. Hal's commitment to putting down the rebellion is complete, regardless of the motives or forces that direct him.

[30] See John C. Robertson, "Hermeneutics of suspicion versus hermeneutics of goodwill" and Ben F. Meyer, "Response," in *Studies in Religion* 8, 4, (Fall 1979): 365–77 (Robertson) and 393–95 (Meyer).

[31] In V, iii, Falstaff tells Hal that he has already "paid Percy" (45), though the Prince doubts him. And later, in V, iv, when the King claims to have seen Prince John holding "Lord Percy at the point," Hal replies, "O, this boy / Lends mettle to us all!" (20–23). See also Empson (43–44).

[32] The King's suspicions are rekindled in *2 Henry IV* when he awakens to find Hal wearing the crown, though the soliloquy that Hal speaks reveals his anxiety about being King rather than his ambition. Furthermore, when the two exchange speeches it is clear that Henry has moved closer to contrition for his past than that expressed in his first meeting with Hal in *1 Henry IV*. Compare *1 Henry IV*, III, ii, and *2 Henry IV*, IV, iv.

[33] I had originally written "where Hal is coming from" in the place now filled by "who Hal is and what he is doing" because the phrase seemed to aptly gather together suggestions about the process of reformation and the notion that Hal's recovery of meaning is a return to older and less amoral ideals. I have since thought better of it and chosen to avoid the slang idiom.

[34] The effect of repetition here seems to be the reverse of what Falstaff had earlier called Hal's "damnable iteration" in alluding to a line which is recognizable from *Proverbs*. See I, ii, 76 and the editor's gloss.

[35] In fact, the final scene of *Henry V*, which centers on

Hal's/Henry's marriage proposal to Katherine of France, may be as enigmatic as his first appearance with Falstaff and Poins in *1 Henry IV,* I, ii.

[36] In his study of Machiavellism, Meinecke notes: "If, after similar acts where idealistic and utilitarian motives might have been operating jointly, anyone were to put the question to himself sincerely as to how far his conduct had been determined by one or another motive, he would in the majority of cases be forced to admit that he was no longer able to distinguish clearly between the two types of motive and that they had intermingled imperceptibly. It is often the case that moral impulses do not make their appearance until after a dispassionate examination has revealed the usefulness and effectiveness of ethical action. . . . Between those sensations and motives which are moral in character and those which are amoral, there too often lie obscure regions of blending and transition; and it can even happen that these obscure regions come to occupy the entire space (Friedrich Meinecke, *Machiavellism,* trans. Douglas Scott [London: Routledge and Kegan Paul, 1924, rpt. 1957] 3–4).

[37] In this connection, see Meinecke's assertion: "The belief that there does exist an absolute, capable of being recovered, is both a theoretical and a practical need; for, without such beliefs, pure contemplation would dissolve into a mere amusement with events, and practical conduct would be irretrievably exposed to all the naturalistic forces of historical life. . . . There are only two points at which the absolute manifests itself unveiled to his gaze: in the pure moral law on the one hand, and in the supreme achievements of art on the other" (433).

10. AMBIGUITIES IN VLADIMIR NABOKOV'S *INVITATION TO A BEHEADING*

Leona Toker

ALMOST EVERY ONE OF Vladimir Nabokov's novels is built on a specific structural principle through which the form and the thematic content are adjusted to each other. Nabokov refers to this principle as "the main structural idea" of the book, and the word "idea" suggests that a thematic significance is attached to technique.[1] The implied author does not merely present us with a certain system of values, he acts it out. By implementing his structural idea, he places himself into the role of an agent whose procedures are dictated by his views.

The structural principle of *Invitation to a Beheading* is that of pervasive ambiguity. Using the ambiguity of separate episodes the novelist monitors and shapes our response to the fictional world. Through the ambiguity of the ending he also prods the protagonist into testing such an attitude in action.

The novel starts with a death sentence. The protagonist, Cincinnatus C., has been found guilty of "gnostic turpitude," that is, of a refusal to accept the mundane as the only reality. A gnostic believes in the possible existence of a mysterious, transcendent dimension, which is forever concealed from humans but can be occasionally glimpsed through gaps and tears in the cloak of materiality. A fragment of this spiritual world is buried inside humans; there-

95

fore, they become conscious of the mystery through self-awareness. Nabokov's model of the relationship between the fictional world and the mind of the author is an apt metaphor for this dualistic view of the universe.

The implications of "gnostic turpitude" are dangerous for any totalitarian regime; therefore, the tormentors of Cincinnatus choose to explain his crime as intransparency. The righteous among his fellow citizens pride themselves on being transparent and cannot forgive him for having retained a solid, opaque spiritual core.

The bulk of the narrative is devoted to the conflict between the protagonist's gnostic dignity and his fear of death. His inner life is presented with psychological accuracy, yet the events in which he is forced to participate are devoid of any conventional logic: characters, situations, and themes undergo fantastic transformations, details of the *fabula* conflict with one another, and contiguous scenes turn out to be mutually exclusive. The only way to resolve the contradictions on the literal level would be to ascribe some of the episodes to the protagonist's dreams or hallucinations. The text encourages such a reading to some extent, but never sanctions it completely. This is the recurrent basis of ambiguity.

In each case, however, the ambiguity can be resolved on a figurative level, bringing into relief the political, the philosophical, or the aesthetic significance of a scene.[2] For instance, when Cincinnatus returns from the trial, his jailer Rodion invites him for a waltz. They dance around the corridor and glide back into the cell, and then Cincinnatus regrets "that the swoon's friendly embrace [has] been so brief."[3] It is not clear whether the whole episode is part of the exhausted man's nightmare or whether we are to take its absurdities at face value and conclude that the swoon has been caused by whirling in the arms of an ill-smelling partner. No amount of literary detection can settle this point, so we have no choice but to treat it as irrelevant and to concentrate on the moral rather than on the literal significance of the action. Cincinnatus is still accepting invitations; the surrogate friendliness of his jailers does not yet repel him. He has a long way to travel.

Similar local effects are produced by other instances of ambiguity. When Cincinnatus is shown leaving prison, walking through the town, coming home, reaching the door of his room, and then entering his prison cell through this door (18-20), it does not matter whether he is supposed to be awake or asleep while undergoing this experience. What matters is the suggestion that his jail is not confined to the fortress on the hill: he is a prisoner in his home, in his society, in literary history, in material existence itself.[4] An additional reminder of the metaphoric function of the fortress comes in another ambiguous episode. In the hope of getting a look through the window of his cell, Cincinnatus moves a table toward it and climbs up, but the view is still inaccessible. The only thing that he can see is an inscription made by a previous frustrated prisoner. He is taken down by Rodion, only to find out, on trying to move the table for the hundredth time, "that the legs [have] been bolted down for ages" (30). Yet we cannot say that he has dreamed of moving the table because in a later scene Rodion recounts that event to the prison director, distorting, however, some of the details. Once more the contradictions can be resolved only on the symbolic plane: there are no physical approaches to the view of the beyond—other people have tried and failed before Cincinnatus.

One last example of this kind: At about the middle of the novel Cincinnatus discovers the liberating effect of his growing contempt for his oppressors. Up to this point his written ramblings have reflected a confused and agonized mind; now, however, he achieves a degree of lucidity. He remembers—or imagines (this is the basis for the ambiguity of the episode)—himself as a schoolboy, sitting on a windowsill upstairs and watching other children engaged in a tedious, structured game in the yard. He is surprised by an angry teacher who tries to chase him off the windowsill. Instead of walking into the room, Cincinnatus steps outside, and in defiance of the law of gravity, remains transfixed in the air.[5] We never learn what is supposed to have happened next because at that moment the jailer steps in and switches off the light in the cell, plunging Cincinnatus and his unfinished manuscript into darkness. We are again suspended between our wish to account for the episode as the product of the protagonist's inspired imagination and the absence of hard, textual evidence that might sanction this view. On the literal level the only available conclusion is that an insight does not mature because it is cut short by the jailer. To reinterpret this in terms of political allegory, a tyrant cannot control the direction of a man's thought, but he can put an end to thought by physical intervention.

In all the above episodes, and in others like them, there remain gaps in the literal plane, in what Barthes would call the code of actions or the proairetic code, the other four codes of a work of fiction being the semic, the symbolic, the hermeneutic, and the cultural.[6] Other layers of meaning, political, philosophical, or aesthetic as the case might be, transpire through these gaps—just as mystery itself shines through the ruptures in the frustrating, familiar reality.[7] Cincinnatus undergoes a series of shocks that gradually annul his commitment to environment. These events—whether actual, imagined, or dreamed—mark important stages in his development, as well as in the development of the reader's response. Ambiguity encourages the reader to imitate the protagonist's salutary contempt for the world around him because it is with a conscious gesture that we as readers waive the literal for the sake of the figurative, and shift our attention to the multilevel allegories of the novel. Such an attitude is detached yet profoundly human: the nature of the protagonist's experience takes precedence over its sources. In Nabokov's short story "That in Aleppo once . . . " the narrator's wife is a compulsive liar, yet her tales evoke the same kind of response in the listeners as if they had been truthful. In most cases they are morally correct, even though they contradict one another and distort the facts of "reality."

This is especially true of *Invitation to a Beheading*. Cincinnatus finds out that he can escape his predicament only by denying that it is real. The novelist, however, knows this all along; therefore, he uses ambiguity in order to knock the foundation from under the outside phenomena that seem real to Cincinnatus. "It is frightening," says the narrator of Nabokov's novel *The Eye*, "when real life suddenly turns out to be a dream, but how much more frightening when that which one had thought a dream—fluid and irresponsible—suddenly starts to congeal into reality!"[8] And so the novelist has to prevent the fictional world, into which he has thrust Cincinnatus, from congealing into a semblance of reality. This is not an easy task. Despite grotesque imagery and serene absurdities, the social setting of the novel keeps gaining substance because we know that certain historical events—the novel, in effect, relies on our response to this part of its cultural code. Therefore, an arsenal of local ambiguities is brought into action in order to render the story as "fluid and irresponsible" as a dream.

Thus the cumulative effect of ambiguity is that of emphasis on the dreamlike insubstantiality of the fictional world. This tendency is carried to an extreme in the last scene of the novel, where ambiguity reaches its climax.

The scene is set around the scaffold. Having already kneeled by the block, Cincinnatus gets up and calmly walks away, wrecking the whole routine. The setting then collapses like cheap decor, and all that remains of the fictional world is a jumble of "rags, chips of painted wood, bits of gilded plaster, pasteboard bricks, posters." Amidst this stage disaster, Cincinnatus "[makes] his way in that direction where, to judge by the voices, [stand] beings akin to him" (223).

Critical literature contains conflicting accounts of this ending. Some commentators, for instance Hyman, hold that it is the soul of the beheaded Cincinnatus making its exit to a different dimension.[9] Others, like Pifer, Stuart, Dillard, and Morton, note that the execution never takes place.[10] The text, however, lends little support to either view, and scholars like Khodasevich, Moynahan, and Peterson do not fail to notice the ambiguity of the passage.[11]

This ambiguity stems largely from the presence of clues that may be read in mutually exclusive ways. The most prominent of such doubly-directed clues is the protest of the headsman's assistant when Cincinnatus declines, so to say, the invitation to his own beheading.[12] "Come back," cries the jailer, "lie down—after all, you were lying down, everything was ready, everything was finished" (223). This may mean that the execution has taken place and that the jailer is distressed on seeing that he has no control of the victim's soul. On the other hand, this may mean that Cincinnatus keeps his life because his tormentors lose power over him as soon as he refuses to play by their rules. The latter reading is not allegorical: in the magic world of *Invitation,* figures of speech and figures of thought are constantly realized in *fabula* situations. On the literal plane, the two implications of the jailer's utterance are in conflict, but on the moral plane, they are in harmony: both continue themes that intertwine throughout the novel.[13]

Another cause of ambiguity is the presence of clues with conflicting connotations. For instance, the protagonist's movements away from the block are presented in a concrete visual manner: he stands up, looks around, walks down the step, and over the debris. In the last sentence of the novel, however, his motions lose their visual quality, while the "voices" that mark his direction seem to have supernatural overtones. Consistently, the text tells us that Cincinnatus goes towards "beings" rather than "people" akin to himself.

To complicate the situation, the text also contains singly-directed clues that not only support one hypothesis but deny the other. Thus, when Cincinnatus rises from the block, the headsman's hips are still swinging, as though gathering momentum for the blow that has not yet been dealt. On the other hand, the pale librarian is vomiting in the audience, which suggests that the gory spectacle has taken place. If one wishes to maintain a definite opinion as to whether or not Cincinnatus is beheaded, one has to explain away one of the clues, risking turning it into a loose end. What, then, does happen at the end of *Invitation?*

My contention is that the novelist dismantles the fictional world an instant after Cincinnatus lays his head on the block. He does so because in an earlier scene he has promised his help to the protagonist. Lying in bed after one of his many disappointments, Cincinnatus cried, "Will no one save me?," and as though in answer to his appeal "there fell and bounced on the blanket a large dummy acorn, twice as large as life, splendidly painted a glossy buff, and fitting its cork cup as snugly as an egg" (125–126). This parody of an acorn falls down from the title oak of the pseudo-realistic novel *Quercus* that Cincinnatus has been reading. Unlike the Newtonian apple, it is governed not by the law of gravity, but by that of "involution,"[14]—that is, the author's self-conscious control of the fictional universe. Like the protagonist of *The Eye,* Cincinnatus cannot achieve the desired detachment without some outside help. The novelist, therefore, lends him succor, in an admittedly *deus ex machina* way.

In his lectures on James Joyce, Nabokov maintains that the Nighttown scenes of *Ulysses* are not the hallucinations of either Stephen or Bloom, but the fantasies of the novelist, a "nightmare evolution" of some of the characters, objects, and themes.[15] Nabokov himself does something similar at the end of *Invitation.* Instead of telling us what is supposed to have happened to Cincinnatus, he presents us with his own fantasy—with the fantastic evolution of the theme of the protagonist's double. At the beginning of the novel this double was described as one that "accompanies each of us—you, and me, and him over there—doing what we would like to do at that very moment, but cannot . . ." (25). In the fantasy of the "finale" ("the book itself is dreaming"[16]), the novelist merges Cincinnatus with this imaginary double and thus enables him to defy conventional limitations. Immediately afterwards the novelist takes apart the nightmare setting and smooths the protagonist's exit into that aesthetic "involute abode" where complete novels and their characters properly belong. Cincinnatus is saved by the same "gnostic turpitude" that has brought him to the scaffold. He shares this crime with his creator, a writer whose aesthetics rest on a tentative yet seductive variety of gnostic dualism.

This view of the novel's ending explains but does not resolve the ambiguity. In the fantasy, the pale librarian is still vomiting, yet the headsman still does not seem to have struck, and we have to accept the ambiguity of death as part of the novel's theme. As Moynahan has observed, "death for a gnostic is always ambiguous. On the one hand, it is the toll he pays to materiality, . . . on the other, it is the only viable release from benightedness and into the 'involute abode.'"[17] This is the local effect of the ambiguous ending.

No less important is its contribution to the cumulative effect of ambiguity as the structural principle of the novel. The ambiguous ending underscores the novelist's refusal to present the world of *Invitation* either in realistic or in earnestly supernatural terms because that would have amounted to re-enacting the mistake into which Cincinnatus lapses in his darkest moments—the mistake of treating his oppressors as real and thus granting them existence and power. Thus, through the use of an appropriate structural formula, Nabokov achieves a perfect unity of content and form.

NOTES

[1] Vladimir Nabokov, *Nikolai Gogol* (Norfolk, Conn.: New Directions, 1944) 148.

[2] Julian Moynahan, "A Russian Preface for Nabokov's *Beheading*," *Novel* I (1967–68): 12–18; Robert Alter, *"Invitation to a Beheading:* Nabokov and the Art of Politics" in *Nabokov: Criticism, Reminiscences, Translations and Tributes*, ed. Alfred Appel, Jr. and Charles Newman (Evanston, Ill.: Northwestern University Press, 1970) 41-59; Ludmila A. Foster, "Nabokov's Gnostic Turpitude: The Surrealistic Vision of Reality in *Priglasenie na kazn'*," in *Mnemozina: Studia literaria russica in honorem Vsevolod Setchkarev*, ed. Joachim T. Baer and Norman W. Ingham (München: Wilhelm Fink, 1974) 117–29; Dale E. Peterson, "Nabokov's *Invitation:* Literature as Execution," *PMLA* 96 (1981): 824–36.

[3] Vladimir Nabokov, *Invitation to a Beheading*, trans. Dmitri Nabokov in collaboration with the author (New York: Putnam, 1959) 14. Unless otherwise stated, subsequent references are also quoted from this source.

[4] See also Foster, "Nabokov's Gnostic Turpitude," 123.

[5] Moynahan suggests that the gnostic is not constrained by physical or social laws if he is young enough to forget them (15). This idea, empirically acceptable only in its figurative meaning, is indeed realized in the *fabula* situation.

[6] Roland Barthes, *S/Z*, trans. Richard Miller (New York: Hill and Wang, 1974) 17–19.

[7] Such a local function of ambiguity and of the resulting gaps is analogous to the function of the Marabar mystery in E. M. Forster, *A Passage to India* (New York: Harcourt, Brace and World, 1952) 207–08. It is interesting to observe how closely the gnosticism of *Invitation* comes to the agnosticism of *Passage:*

> If this world is not to our taste, well, at all events there is Heaven, Hell, Annihilation—one or other of these large things, that huge scenic background of stars, fires, blue or black air. All heroic endeavour, and all that is known as art, assumes that there is such a background, just as all practical endeavour, when the world is to our taste, assumes that the world is all.

[8] Vladimir Nabokov, *The Eye*, trans. Dmitri Nabokov in collaboration with the author (New York: Phaedra, 1965) 108.

[9] Edgar Stanley Hyman, "The Handle: *Invitation to a Beheading* and *Bend Sinister*," in Appel and Newman, *Nabokov*, 61.

[10] Richard Dillard, "Not Text, but Texture: The Novels of Vladimir Nabokov," in *The Sounder Few: Essays from the Hollins Critic,* ed. R.H.W. Dillard, George Garrett, and John Rees Moore (Athens: University of Georgia Press, 1971) 143; Donald Morton, *Vladimir Nabokov* (New York: Frederick Ungar, 1974) 40; Dobner Stuart, *Nabokov: The Dimension of Parody* (Baton Rouge: Louisiana State University Press, 1978) 85; Ellen Pifer, *Nabokov and the Novel* (Cambridge, Mass.: Harvard University Press, 1980) 55.

[11] Vladislav Khodasevich, "On Sirin," Appel and Newman, *Nabokov*, 98; Moynahan, 15; Peterson, 833.

[12] For a discussion of singly and doubly-directed clues as causes of ambiguity see Shlomith Rimmon, *The Concept of Ambiguity—The Example of James* (Chicago: University of Chicago Press, 1977) 52–58.

[13] The former of these two themes is more extensively discussed by Pifer, 51–54; the latter by Moynahan, 15 ff.

[14] Alfred Appel, Jr., "Nabokov's Puppet Show," in *The Single Voice*, ed. Jerome Charyn (London: Collier-Macmillan, 1969) 87–93.

[15] Vladimir Nabokov, *Lectures on Literature*, ed. Fredson Bowers (New York: Harcourt Brace Jovanovich, 1980) 350.

[16] Nabokov, *Lectures on Literature,* 350.

[17] "A Russian Preface, " 15.

11. AUTHOR, TEXT, AND SELF IN *BUFFALO BILL AND THE INDIANS*

Robert T. Self

SEYMOUR CHATMAN REMINDS us that "point of view is the physical place or ideological situation or practical life-orientation to which narrative events stand in relation," and thus makes it clear that the meaning of a literary text is situated between values of authorship and readership, of production and consumption, of construction and interpretation.[1] The hermeneutic quest for meaning becomes both a search for an author and a search for a self.

There exists in criticism today "a strong correlation between theories of the self and theories of the text," the text like the human subject "'defined as a locus of relationships' and hence impossible to totalize, to define in any way but as a place of intersection of multiple functions, 'of other voices.'"[2] Perhaps the most postmodern of his films, Robert Altman's *Buffalo Bill and the Indians, or Sitting Bull's History Lesson* (1976) asserts the difficulty of any unified, coherent identity of the self or any unified meaning of a text. William F. Cody's struggle to express himself confronts the competing authors of that self, the babel of voices that authorize Cody as literally a textual other. The reader's struggle to locate meaning in the text similarly engages the multivocular discourse of theory that makes critical comprehension or interpretation a process always in contradiction, perpetually open to change and ambiguity. The film suggests a parallel between the sense of self for William F. Cody and the sense of textual meaning for the film analyst. In the film there is a tension between William F. Cody as an apparently whole individual capable of meaning, knowledge, and action and the image of Buffalo Bill as an ensemble literally of conflicting historical, psychological, and ideological forces, a creation of divers authorial hands and the product of divergent media of communication and art. Cody would claim himself humanistically as the captain of his fate and the master of his soul, but the portrait he sees when he looks in the mirror is a stranger. What the critic also finds when he looks in the text is not an author, what Stephen Heath calls a "function of unity," but a multiplication of authorial voices that establish *Buffalo Bill and the Indians* as a locus of different codes, articulations, contradictions.[3] Moreover, just as Cody endeavors to find continuity within the disorder of his personae, so the analyst finds the ability to interpret diffused by the divergent discourse of film/ literary/narrative theory whose enunciations contradictorily delineate the text and articulate the critic. The self in the text, the text, and the self viewing the text are products of competing authors.

Buffalo Bill is an "interrogative" work "particularly in the absence of a single privileged discourse which contains and places all the others."[4] The historical time presented in the story is 1885 when Cody was thirty-nine, a heavily-coded age of transition in our culture, and a time of literal transition for the Cody of history: It was the first successful year of Buffalo Bill's Wild West Show, marking the transformation of Cody from theatrical performer to the star of a new kind of national entertainment. In 1885 Ned Buntline, the original author of that famous and long-lived dime-novel series, wrote his last Buffalo Bill novel. In the same year Prentiss Ingraham embarked upon a writing career that would produce over two hundred Buffalo Bill dime novels. The success of the Wild West Show in 1885 derived in large part from the crowd-pleasing additions to its company of the sharp-shooter Annie Oakley and the infamous Sioux Indian Chief Sitting Bull, and in larger part from the show-business skill of producer Nate Salsbury and the advertising activity of promoter "Arizona" John Burke. All of these figures appear in the film as sources for the image of Buffalo Bill and are themselves characterized as functions in a larger process of cultural production.

Ned Buntline recounts his first encounter with the young Cody as a predetermined textual idea:

> I ask his name, says Cody, Bill Cody, I says what
> do ya do, says he's a scout and buffalo hunter. Well,

> I'm eager to write about somebody 'cause I got a
> batch of excitin' plots I might take to Hickok but I'm
> mad at him, so I tell the kid from now on his name is
> Buffalo Bill and in six months the whole country's
> gonna know about you. That's all I say and I walk
> away. Sure enough, these stories come out and are a
> big success and the kid comes lookin' for me, scared
> to death about the legends I created but real excited
> with his new fame.[5]

And Buntline's penultimate line in the film claims authority: "Buffalo Bill, it's been the thrill of my life to have invented ya" (138). Throughout the film Buntline appears as a chorus remarking on the differences between his dime-novel image of Buffalo Bill and the emerging show business image: "Profit is all that counts, creative thinking is gone forever" (72) he says to his authorial successor Ingraham. John Burke, on the other hand, proclaims to Buntline, "We've turned the page you were written on" (71). Salsbury's apologia that "we're involved in living American drama, . . . so you can't have anything that isn't authentic, genuine, and real" (8) is also grounded in his own authorial concerns: "All I care about is the Wild West. I'm going to Codyfy the world" (36).

These conflicts over the ownership of the heroic image ultimately involve a conflict between reality and history. History and biography become the stuff of popular entertainment which acquires the facts of reality and repackages them as show business in a portrayal of the way Carl Malmgren says postmodern stories deal with history: "It is as if the fictionist intends to 'eat' history—consume, digest, and regurgitate it—before history eats him."[6] The reality of the "actual" West lies outside the Fort Ruth headquarters of the Wild West Show, the show already a historicizing of the place and an "imaging" of frontiersmen like Cody.

When the conflict between Cody and Sitting Bull begins, the Indians, too, leave that reality out there (the *Ding an sich*, an unknowable wilderness) and enter the three-ring circus of history, of narrative, of explanatory discourse. Within the competition to enunciate Buffalo Bill as the hero of various western stories, William F. Cody struggles with Sitting Bull to authorize his version of history and thus to valorize his own sense of self. Yet the nature of that external reality and that past (and that self) is as different and as puzzling as death itself, with which, throughout the film, it is associated.

Cody enters the competition to narrativize himself as Buffalo Bill, then, out of necessity—his need to assert his own reality, or as he claims, his "better sense of history." "Everything historical is mine," he exclaims (18). His uncertain sense of self is revealed by the exaggerations of his stories. Of three separate accounts in the film of the death of a Cheyenne war chief, Cody's is the most egotistical and preposterously farfetched. Buntline observes ironically: "no ordinary man'd realize what tremendous profit could be had by presentin' the truth as if it was just a pack o' lies with witnesses" (101). Narrative as a form of ego-defense characterizes the conflict between Cody's and Sitting Bull's accounts of the Battle of the Little Big Horn. In Cody's version, Buffalo Bill rides heroically onto the scene to avenge a cowardly killing of Custer by Sitting Bull. Sitting Bull responds with a story of how his braves retaliated against Custer's cowardly killing of Indian women and children. Significantly, both men sing their own praises in verse. Cody recites a poem about himself:

> Nature's proud she made this man—
> This man, Buffalo Bill.
> For it's always been his plan
> To save others from the kill. (40)

Sitting Bull declaims:

> My Father has given me this land.
> In protecting it I have had a hard time.
> The rivers flow with the blood of my people.
> The winds blow the echoes of lies.
> The white man has stolen the truth.
> My desire is to love all nature.
> My desire is to be loved by all that
> is pure and good. (91–92)

In these heroic descriptions, the "real" dies to a fictive history. Buntline claims that "Bill's dying inside to be a hero for all the eastern behaved" (63). Sitting Bull claims that "history is nothing more than disrespect for the dead" (87).

The contest for the ownership of history and the authorship of Buffalo Bill's image is revealed as indigenous to contradictions normally smoothed over as an ideological strategy. There is a telling exchange between the producer and the promoter of the show as they watch Cody ride to greet Sitting Bull: "That's my star," says Salsbury. "He belongs to all of us, Nate," corrects Burke. "Our Star," responds Salsbury. Then they turn to watch Cody and say, "America's star!" Cody's sense of himself as a heroic subject as well as the show-business sense of him generated by various authors are conveyed as ideological constructs. The film presents the conflicting images of Cody and Buffalo Bill as responses to needs larger than personal. The opening scene of the movie, depicting an Indian attack on a settler's cabin, first presents itself as a kind of movie reality before a zoom out reveals the scene as a rehearsal for the show. This interplay between presentation and representation underlines the ironically ideological import of the voice-over:

> These brave souls survived not only nature but the savage instincts of man, paving the way for the heroes that endured. Welcome then to the real events enacted by men and women of the American frontier, to whose courage, strength and, above all, faith, this piece of our history is dedicated. (5)

The worth of the Wild West Show's demonstration of western heroism merits a command performance before the President of the United States *and* on his wedding night at that. Buffalo Bill promotes the "Star-Spangled Banner" as a new national anthem, and his role as "national entertainer" establishes him at the head of "America's national family" where blacks, Mexicans, Indians, and whites live together harmoniously as they perform dramas of white aggression and racial superiority. Metaphorically in the film William F. Cody must accede to, must die for the heroic image of Buffalo Bill in the ideological drama of cowboys and Indians, just as Sitting Bull must literally die in order for his role as villain to be portrayed in that drama. The "real" individuals die for their fictional functions as authored by the dominant mythology. Whatever his other roles require, this myth asserts: "It's men like you that have made this country what it is, Buffalo Bill" (133).

Politically the film bares this ideological formulation, but it does not in the process restore any sense of individual authenticity. Rather "Robert Altman" becomes another author function in the fictive reconstruction of historic personality. As the image of Buffalo Bill is situated within an intertextual space designated by "the western," then the tension William F. Cody/Buffalo Bill is further compounded by Altman's authorial manipulation of the taken-for-granted aspects of three generic patterns. The mythological founding of a new civilization that authorized Buffalo Bill in films like *The Plainsman* (1937) is strikingly conveyed in the iconography of a fort with flag flying at the edge of a lovely Rocky Mountain valley. But Fort Ruth, here, is a circus headquarters. The ideological expression of manifest destiny implicit in *Pony Express* (1953) is conveyed here as racist superiority. Cody tells Sitting Bull in his dream that "The difference 'tween a white man and a Injun in *all* situations is . . . a Injun is red!" (141). And the ritualistic resolution of the conflict between the individual and society in William Wyler's film *Buffalo Bill* (1944), and so many other westerns is, here, completely displaced by the multiplication of conflicting individualities in Cody. As in nearly every other depiction of Buffalo Bill or Wild Bill Hickok or Wyatt Earp—the gallery of historic individuals that fills our western stories—Altman authors the heroic personality under the influence of changing cultural values. Adopting Arthur Kopit's play, *Indians,* Altman joins the ritual of demythology: earlier, popular romanticizing of Buffalo Bill gives way to a Bicentennial need to debunk the western hero and cast him as a villain in the genocide of the Indians, here re-mythologized as the noble savage. In e.e. cummings' critical query, "Buffalo Bill's defunct. . . . How do you like your blue-eyed boy now, Mr. Death."

A significant function of the conflicting voices articulating Buffalo Bill is the psychological formation that they motivate. The film constantly focuses the issue of personality by contrasting shots of William F. Cody and images of Buffalo Bill. There are a wide variety of portraits, photographs, billboards, tents, placards, and banners bearing his name and face; at two key moments Cody directly confronts those images. These confrontations are commentaries on the parallels between the psychological development of the individual and the representation of the subject in film. The whole movie might be seen as an inversion of the ideological placement of the subject as a whole, the center of consciousness and discourse firmly fixed by the authority of some specular other. The first instance occurs when Sitting Bull leaves the Wild West headquarters and enters the wilderness; as Cody rides off in his "real" jacket to hunt the Indians, Buntline in a voice-over marks the contrast between the man and the show-business image:

> When Bill's dressed for a ride and mounted on that
> high-steppin' stallion o' his, any doubts concernin'
> his legends are soon forgot. Yes, Bill's fine physical
> portrait hides any faults his mind might possess.
> (110)

Upon his empty-handed return, Cody stops in front of an imposing portrait of himself that poignantly jars against the weakness of his actual performance. The film presents three shots: of Cody looking up at the image, of the image alone, then of Cody alone—a rendering of the classical point of view structure which graphically indicates the distance between Cody and Buffalo Bill, which indicates his awareness of that separation, and which represents the mirror stage of personal development. It is a moment when the symbolic systems of his existence become transparent to the dependency of the ego upon the presence of the other, the moment of self-perception with its attendant splitting of the *I* that is perceived from the *I* that does the perceiving. It is a silent moment that captures the separation between the subject of an enunciation, here in the portrait, and the enunciating subject, that "contradiction between the conscious self, the self which appears in its own discourse, and the self which is only partially represented there."[7]

The second event occurs as the climactic sequence in the film. Prior to the President's visit to the Wild West, an event predicted by Sitting Bull's dream, Buntline tells us that Cody never dreams, that he's "just a sleeper." But that night after the show and the departure forever of Buntline, his "first" author, Cody finally dreams, and the dream involves a sublimation of William F. Cody to the image function of show business. The dream reflects the unconscious process which itself "is constructed in the moment of entry into the symbolic order, simultaneously with the construction of the subject."[8] The dream at once represents the subject as a relation and the identification process involved in his role as a show-business star, as a subject for another signifier: "I got people with . . . *no lives*

... livin' *through me!*" (40). In his dream he looks up at the image of that star—astride his white horse, resplendent in beaded buckskins, golden hair streaming down—then turns and looks directly into the camera (now both spectating and enunciating subject) and says: "My god, he's riding that horse well, and if he ain't, how come all y'all took him for a king?" The moment at once asserts the splitting of the ego and the displacement of the unstable subject into the relational system of the symbolic, particularly here the ideological function of popular entertainment to establish a unified, coherent subject position. Buntline earlier had asserted that "Injuns gear their lives to dreams" and compared Sitting Bull's dreaming to Cody's actions: "Now, I ain't an expert on the subject, but what Bull does is sure a hell of a lot cheaper than mounting a Wild West show, which is just dreamin' out loud" (123). The show business, the dream, the western narrative are forms of the symbolic order which work to control the essential discontinuities, the inherent instability of the ego. Here the film reveals the conditions of subjectivity as the purchase of meaning, of unity, and of heroic action at the expense of the heterogenous, the unconscious, the psychologically unsaid.

The next and last scene of the film occurs five years later. Buffalo Bill is a star, the Wild West Show a success. Cody, metaphorically, and Sitting Bull, literally, are dead as enunciating subjects, but they live on as the subjects enunciated by the narrative relationship of cowboy and Indian. As Cody says in his dream to the Chief: "In one hundred years . . . in other people's shows . . . I'm still *Buffalo Bill* . . . star! You're still . . . *The Injun!*" (141). Indeed, Burke exclaims at the end of the film: "Sitting Bull's not dead. Not as long as Buffalo Bill's alive to kill him in every show!" (149).

The opening sentence of the film's script captures the magnification of this symbolic function and the split between the *I* of the discourse and the *I* of the speaker: "I, William F. Cody, Buffalo Bill [Paul Newman] to most of you, was the undisputed lion of the Show Business in 1885" (1). From the outset the film works to deconstruct the ideological and psychological projections of a stable subjectivity in mass media entertainment. As Bill Nichols notes:

> Perception is indeed purposive and serves larger social purposes than individual survival. It helps mold the very image we have of ourselves as

subjects. At the same time, however, it helps obscure
that larger sense of self beyond the conscious self
that harbors the rules-of-the-game, the codes that,
among other things, weave the web in which the ego
is centered.[9]

At the self-reflexive level of the discourse as well as the dramatic level of the story, William F. Cody is a subject situated by the
authorial voices of the mass media. Robert Altman's retelling of the
Buffalo Bill story not only conveys the loss of identity that accompanies the transmutation of individual personality into entertainment star, but his recreation of the western hero indicates that
this transition in identity with its concomitant distortion, or displacement, of an antecedent reality inevitably characterizes the evolution of mythical heroes, who are always representatives for the
writers and producers who articulate that identity. We not only
watch a minor frontier hero named William Cody becoming a show-
business deity manufactured and manipulated by Ned Buntline,
John Burke, Nate Salsbury, and Prentiss Ingraham, we also watch
the process of manufacturing as Altman enlarges the camera perspective to include his film as part of the manipulation that constantly reinterprets history. Just as Nate Salsbury presents the Ned
Buntline–Prentiss Ingraham creation of Buffalo Bill's Wild West,
starring William F. Cody, so Dino DeLaurentiis presents Robert
Altman's "ABSOLUTELY ORIGINAL AND HEROIC ENTER-
PRISE OF INIMITABLE LUSTER," *Buffalo Bill and the Indians,*
starring Paul Newman. William Frederick Cody is constrained by a
variety of subject positions variously articulated by the demands of
history, of popular mythology, of psychology, of economics, as
well as of the media.

To discuss systematically these perspectives is to belie much
of the indeterminacy of *Buffalo Bill and the Indians* as an interrogative text which "disrupts the unity of the reader by discouraging
identification with a unified subject of the enunciation. The position
of the 'author' inscribed in the text, if it can be located at all, is seen
as questioning or as literally contradictory."[10] Indeed, a large part of
the power of this film rests in its depiction of authorship and ego as
heterogenous and discontinuous.

William F. Cody longs to assert himself without contradiction
(in two senses of that word). The penultimate image of the film—a

slow, low angle zoom in to Cody's face as he stands triumphantly over the body of Sitting Bull in the Wild West arena—would seem to indicate the merging of Cody with the publicity images of Buffalo Bill, had not the film made clear the multiple identities which the symbolic of narrative performance seeks to contain. The personality of William Cody/Buffalo Bill is divided between perceived and perceiver, never authored so much by himself as by an other. And the cacophony of voices that authorize the subject position "Buffalo Bill" (and indeed "Robert Altman" as well) is paradigmatic of the critical viewer as subject to the authors of a text, as inscribed in the story of criticism by the narration of dominant theorists.[11]

The contemporary critical viewer, when looking for meaning, for an interpretation, discovers a multiplicity of subject positions within the text which echo a similar contest of critical voices that situate his viewing. As John Caughie writes, "the crack in the singular text's self-containment is opened wider by questions of subjects other than the purely textual subject—social subjects, sexual subjects, historical subjects—subjects who are constituted in a plurality of discourses (in an intertextuality of other texts) of which the single text is only one moment."[12]

The current film analyst is aware that the death of the author has meant the birth of many authors, the death of the self supplanted by many selves. *Buffalo Bill and the Indians* designates "BB" as the site of conflicting codes of meaning, and the film scholar is similarly aware of him/her self, academic critic, as the site of numerous codes. Culler states:

> But as meaning is explained in terms of systems of signs—systems which the subject does not control —the subject is deprived of his role as source of meaning. I know a language, certainly, but since I need a linguist to tell me what it is that I know, the status and the nature of the "I" which knows is called into question: "The goal of the human sciences," says Levi-Strauss, "is not to constitute man but to dissolve him." Although they begin by making man an object of knowledge, these disciplines find, as their work advances, that the self is dissolved as its various functions are ascribed to impersonal systems which operate through it.[13]

A range of responses to this situation is represented by the film. At one end of the spectrum it is possible to see William Cody succumb to the public image of himself demanded by the arena, offered by the symbolic. But at the other end the film reflects a series of narrative conflicts with little confluence and impossible to resolve. Culler describes this array of response thus:

> What Kant calls the 'mathematical sublime' arises out of cognitive exhaustion, when confronting sheer proliferation, with no hope of bringing a long series or a vast scattering under some sort of conceptual unity, the mind experiences a 'momentary checking of its vital powers,' followed by a compensatory positive movement, and exultation in its own confrontation of the unmasterable.[14]

One approach to the impasse described by Culler is a kind of rage for order. A major paradox of deconstructive criticism, for instance, is the reconstitution of the heterogenous text under a more inclusive definition. What, then, allows us to comprehend the contradictions in a text, the signifying patterns of a text in a historical context, the mix of codes, structures, and languages in a text is a theory of the subject. An inevitable effect of the symbolic is to naturalize the process of signification and thus to assert the legality of its discourse, its efforts to control the differences, the desires, the absences of the imaginary.

At the other end of this spectrum, however, is the postmodern response which accepts the plural text in all its ambiguity and indeterminacy. In the political analysis of *Buffalo Bill and the Indians* which was published in *Jump Cut,* Janey Place praised the film for achieving a Brechtian distanciation from bourgeois values but felt the film failed to achieve Marcuse's "hope for radical art that would involve the passions of the viewer and liberate his/her sensual feelings which are so repressed in our culture."[15] But within the context of Kant's "mathematical" sublime a very sensuous possibility exists for identifying with a film like *Buffalo Bill*. Its humorous, multiple addressing of subjects mirrors the critic variously situated by the competing voices of critical discourse; the struggle for a fictive or academic self "whole beyond confusion" is replaced by a liberating recognition of many selves in process, even when one of these identities may seem for an ironic moment fixed by the signifying chain. Altman's film is ultimately about the pressures that continually unfix the subject in a context that demands stability. In this sense his film evokes the critical situation described by Ihab Hassan:

> It is a movement that explores the subjective life, the silent structure of language and of conciousness, and implicates criticism into a wider experience, the fantasy of culture. It is a movement, beyond the control of the art object, toward the openness, and even the gratuitousness—gratuitous is free—of existence. Perhaps it is even a movement toward the generalization of our attention in an age that heralds universal leisure, the end of specialization—a movement, therefore, that seeks to adapt the literary response to new conditions of survival.[16]

NOTES

[1] Seymour Chatman, *Story and Discourse* (Ithaca, New York: Cornell, 1978) 153.

[2] Susan R. Suleiman, "Introduction: Varieties of Audience-Oriented Criticism," *The Reader in the Text* (Princeton, New Jersey: Princeton, 1980) 41.

[3] Stephen Heath, "Comment on the 'Idea of Authorship,' " in *Theories of Authorship*, ed. John Caughie (London: Routledge and Kegan Paul, 1980) 217.

[4] Catherine Belsey, *Critical Practice* (London: Methuen, 1980) 92.

[5] Alan Rudolph and Robert Altman, *Buffalo Bill and the Indians* (New York: Bantam, 1976) 22. Unless otherwise stated, subsequent references are also quoted from this source.

[6] Carl Darryl Malmgren, *Fictional Space in Modernist and Postmodernist Fiction* (Lewisburg, PA: Bucknell, 1985) 171.

[7] Belsey, 64.

[8] Belsey, 65.

[9] Bill Nichols, *Ideology and Image* (Bloomington: Indiana, 1981) 33.

[10] Belsey, 91.

[11] Robert Self, "Robert Altman and the Theory of Authorship," *Cinema Journal* 25 (Fall 1985): 3–11.

[12] John Caughie, "Fiction of the Author/Author of the Fiction," in *Theories of Authorship*, ed. John Caughie (London: Routledge and Kegan Paul, 1980) 206.

[13] Jonathan Culler, *The Pursuit of Signs* (Ithaca, New York: Cornell, 1981) 33.

[14] Culler, 110.

[15] Janey Place, " 'Buffalo Bill and the Indians': Welcome to Show Business," *Jump Cut* 23 (October 1980): 22.

[16] Ihab Hassan, *Paracriticisms* (Urbana: Illinois, 1975) 27–28.

12. DREAM AND THE AMBIGUITY OF *CITY OF WOMEN*

Robert T. Eberwein

THE FORM AND CONTENT of Federico Fellini's *City of Women* (1980) have provoked varying and generally unsympathetic comments from the critics. Some inveigh against the director's use of dream as a means of organizing the narrative.[1] Others attack Fellini for his hostile anti-feminism, although one writer thinks the film has a "feminist orientation," and at least one feminist, Molly Haskell, sees the film delivering "a muscled broadside at archaic male chauvinists."[2] The diametrically opposed views on the issue of feminism suggest the presence of ambiguity within the work, but because the ambiguity has been misunderstood, evaluation of the film, even when positive, has been somewhat misguided. The purpose of this essay is to argue that by examining the relation of the dream which informs the narrative to the nature of the cinematic process, we can understand what Fellini actually thinks about his hero and about feminism.

Virtually all of the film represents the dream of its hero Snaporaz (Marcello Mastroianni). After falling asleep on a train, he dreams that a beautiful woman (Bernice Stegers) enters his compartment. When she leaves the train, after kissing him passionately, Snaporaz pursues her in a quest to regain this being who seems to be the perfect woman. His adventures in search of her lead him to a hotel populated by a convention of feminists, most of whom are fervently anti-male, where he is ridiculed; to a greenhouse where he is almost raped by a huge woman (the coal-stoker for the hotel); to a

117

lonely road where he is threatened by violent teenaged girls; to the mansion of an aging sybarite, Signor Züberkock (Ettore Manni), where a party celebrating the host's final sexual conquest is interrupted by feminists in S.S. uniforms; and finally to a trial—his own—where he is found innocent of his chauvinist sins and allowed to go free. As he prepares to leave, he enters the cupola of an immense balloon which is in the form of a young girl (Donatella Damiani) he has encountered throughout his adventures; the girl herself, dressed in a guerrilla outfit, shoots down the balloon. Snaporaz awakes from his fall and discovers himself back in the train compartment where he finds his wife, Elena (Anna Prucnal), and other women from the dream. They laugh at the mystified hero who seems to be as disoriented by reality as he has been in the dream.

This brief summary does not convey the humor or complexity of Fellini's inventiveness throughout the film, nor does it suggest the extent to which the women Snaporaz meets continue to reappear in his adventures, sometimes unchanged—his wife, for example—and sometimes transformed like Donatella, who, besides appearing as the guerrilla, is also a roller skating instructor and a showgirl.

However, Fellini's use of the dream, with its own mad logic, is an essential condition of the film's narrative form for two important reasons. First, the content of the dream can be seen as a projection of the dreamer's mind. In Jungian terms, for example, the women might be seen as constituting the collective *animae* of Snaporaz, those parts of him which are female. Fellini himself, no stranger to Jungian analysis, has said, in fact, that even Donatella, who shoots down the balloon, is part of Snaporaz: "The film is really a dream, and as in a dream, everything is the dreamer."[3] In Freudian terms, the aging Züberkock could be seen as an embodiment of one aspect of an anxiety dream, revealing Snaporaz's fear of impotency and death. The various falls he suffers in the dream (from the balloon, down the stairs while roller skating, and down the chute after he crawls along the floor in Züberkock's home) might be connected to Freud's comments on the re-experiencing of infantile sensations in dreams.

The dream is even more significant for a second reason since what the hero encounters during the oneiric experience are images, the same kind of insubstantial images we know in the cinema. Now is not the time to repeat the standard comparisons or describe the complex affinities between film and dream that have been urged over the years by critics and theorists. Suffice it to say that the dreaming mind, like that of the observer watching the cinema, loses itself in a realm of images. Common to both is the ontological status of these images which often are themselves the product of operations involving construction (Freud's condensation in the dreamwork) or what Perkins calls "fictionalizing" (the manner by which viewers construct a reality implied but not defined by the assemblage of shots—the Mosjukhim experiment, for example).[4]

We might consider, in this regard, two quotations: one from Kuleshov describing a montage experiment and one from Fellini.

> Kuleshov: In [this] experiment we interchanged people themselves. I shot a girl sitting before her mirror, painting her eyelashes and brows, putting on lipstick and slipper. By montage alone we were able to depict the girl, just as in nature, but in actuality she did not exist, because we shot the lips of one woman, the legs of another, the back of a third, and the eyes of a fourth. We spliced the pieces together in a predetermined relationship and created a totally new person. This particular example . . . demonstrated that the entire power of cinematic effect is in montage.[5]

> Fellini: *City of Women* is really a film about the cinema, about the cinema seen as a woman, the cinema seen throught its femininity, through the masturbatory discovery of its femininity. . . . I think the cinema is a woman by virtue of its ritualistic nature. This uterus which is the theatre, the fetal darkness, the apparitions—all create a projected relationship, we project ourselves onto it. We become involved in a series of vicarious transpositions, and we make the screen assume the character of what we expect of it, just as we do with women, upon whom we impose ourselves. Woman being a series of projections invented by man. In history, she became our dream image. . . [The film] is about one man . . . who invents woman. She is his metaphor, his obscurity, the part of himself he doesn't know . . . .

119

It is clear that he knows nothing about women, he isn't able to create in his imagination/film a single outstanding, real person, which is why the film has no female protagonist. There are just thousands of faces, of mouths, of smiles, of looks, of voices. My feminist critics are even now saying that in the whole film there isn't one real woman. Of course there isn't. There wasn't meant to be. Because if there was a real woman, it would have been useless to make the film.[6]

The parallel, if not exactly precise, is nonetheless striking. For Kuleshov, montage, the basis of cinema, becomes a way of creating a woman who does exist. The "Woman" is constituted by a series of fragments, parts of other women abstracted and then synthesized. Fellini's Snaporaz, who is searching for the ideal woman, encounters faces, smiles, mouths, looks, voices, fragments, images of an ultimate reality. In both cases, Woman is unreal, the product of the director's (and dreamer's) manipulation of images. Kuleshov constructed a woman to show what cinema consisted of—montage. Fellini's cinema *is* Woman, the assembled parts of all women.

The quotations, especially the latter one from Fellini, seem, in a curious (even perverse) way, to offer theoretical confirmation of the arguments advanced by a feminist critic such as Mulvey who says,

The man controls the film phantasy and also emerges as the representative of power in a further sense: as the bearer of the look of the spectator, transferring it behind the screen to neutralise the extradiegetic tendencies represented by the woman as spectacle. This is made possible through the processes set in motion by structuring the film around a main controlling figure with whom the spectator can identify. As the spectator identifies with the main male protagonist, he projects his look onto that of his like, his screen surrogate, so that the power of the male protagonist as he controls events coincides with the active power of the erotic look, both giving a satisfying sense of omnipotence.[7]

And one way that this omnipotence is maintained, various feminists have argued, is through the fragmentation and fetishizing of woman's image.

The quotation from Fellini seems to bear out the charges of the feminists, particularly when we consider two key scenes of the dream occurring during the visit to Züberkock. The sybarite's home is decorated in what can only be described as period sex-shop: erotic statuary, pictures that give French kisses, etc. Two of his *objets d'art* are of particular significance: a bust of his dead mother mounted decorously and reverently on a pedestal, and a picture gallery. The latter includes dozens of photographs of his previous conquests. When Snaporaz presses a button under each picture, he hears a recording of the woman's moans and cries, which she made while making love to Züberkock. In the gallery, then, Woman is represented by a series of smiling photographs; they are fragmented memories, framed, fixed like hunter's trophies, audio-visual mementos of male power. Even in the absence of the women, Züberkock and Snaporaz can demonstrate their potency by making them the subjects of their gazes and by listening to their orgasmic cries. Such images and cries signify the females' submission to the male. Why is each woman smiling? Because Züberkock gave her pleasure.

During the party, Snaporaz meets Elena who gives him a tongue lashing for his indifference, and then encounters Donatella and another young woman with whom he performs a charming dance routine. After they put him to bed, Elena appears, alternately screaming in mock orgasmic rapture and wailing arias before she falls asleep. Having heard a noise, Snaporaz leaves their bed and crawls along the floor to investigate. He falls down a chute, and, during his descent, he encounters scenic representations of his past, specifically those of a sexual nature. One such memory is of himself as a teenager: we see a large group of boys on an immense bed under a billowing sheet. They are masturbating as they watch a screen on which we see projected clips of films depicting a silent heroine, Greta Garbo, Marlene Dietrich, and Mae West. These images epitomize what male directors have done by way of imaging women. Unlike the scene in *Amarcord* (1973) in which we watch a shaking automobile filled with boys who masturbate and call out names of actresses and local women, we see here the images of the women who stimulate the youths. Cinema/Woman/Image—unable to possess the signified, the boys interact by means of sexual fantasy with the signifier. All they know is the signifier, the image which they control with their gaze. That is all Züberkock knows, or Snaporaz, in the gallery.

It seems as if Fellini had set out to illustrate the truth of the feminists' position. These scenes, rather than those of the feminists' convention, are the truly crucial ones in the film. In them Fellini demonstrates that what feminists have said is correct. He *does* make women out of and into images; in so doing, he fails to confront Woman. Cinema is Woman without Women. Herein lies the film's ambiguity. His hero takes something from every woman he knows and, as if in illustration of the process of condensation in dreams or montage in cinema, assembles a being like Kuleshov's woman— equally unreal. But Fellini's depiction of this behavior is significant, an admission which he underscores by presenting both the scene in the picture gallery and in the scene of the youths. When one looks only at the results of the telling, the film seems sexist. But when one considers what Fellini has done in these particular scenes, the film does not appear to me to be championing male sexuality.

The hero encounters Woman in her various roles: wife, mother, whore. By the end of his dream, he has attempted to fuse these images into one essential image combining the physical and moral aspects of the women he has seen. These combine in the balloon image of Donatella—part attractive young woman, part madonna (complete with halo). This image, which lifts the cupola, will take him away to safety; when he sees it, he believes he has found paradise, a smiling and benign force who will carry him off into the clouds. But he discovers that this perfect amalgam of Woman cannot sustain him. The balloon literally and metaphorically bursts, shot down by the "real" Donatella, and drops him back into reality. He awakens from a dream that he could ever find such perfections. Even more, he awakens to the reality of Woman's mystery. What *do* they know? Why are the women in the compartment smiling?

We can compare this truly awakened Snaporaz with other Fellini heroes in order to determine how his experiences suggest a new direction for Fellini. For example, *The Temptations of Dr. Antonio* (1961), a generally neglected work, presents Mazzuolo, a prudish hypocrite, clearly the butt of Fellini's irony, who conducts a one-man campaign to have a gigantic poster of Anita Ekberg removed from his view. The poster shows her advertising: DRINK

MORE MILK. The image combines the suggestion of mothering with the image of woman as whore (Swedish sex bomb)— an image which Fellini had helped to solidify in *La Dolce Vita* (1960). In a fantasy/dream caused by Cupid, the prude encounters her as a live being who pursues him through the streets of Rome and begins to take off her clothes. It is exactly what Mazzuolo does and does not want: his repressed sexual desires conflict with his puritanical code. He goes mad at the end and is led away. Comical as the film is, it nonetheless displays Fellini reveling in the "image" in a way that bears noting in comparison to *City of Women*. In the earlier film, what is affirmed is not so much the power of love (as the use of Cupid would suggest), but the exploitation of the image itself. Ekberg is a threat to the hero when she steps down from the poster, but by the end, there she is, back up on the poster—indeed, given the proportions of the poster, back on what looks like a Cinemascope screen. The film's operation confirms woman as image, as object appropriate for the gaze.

In *8 1/2* (1962), Guido's creative block, linked to a mid-life crisis, is caused in part by his inability to control the various images which appear in his dreams, memories, and fantasies. Still, he is not totally overwhelmed by them. It is useful to recall his memory of himself as a child being tucked into bed by adoring females (nurse, mother) and the security he feels, and compare it to Snaporaz here. When the latter is tucked in by Donatella, he spends a restless night: woman no longer comforts him but instead screeches arias at him. In the harem fantasy, Guido's retinue attempts to revolt but is quickly put down as he lashes out at them with his whip. Here, Snaporaz cannot control real women, a fact signalled by his increasingly incongruous and ridiculous appearance in their midst at the convention on roller skates, and, even more tellingly, with the teenaged girls on the road.

In *Casanova* (1976), with its repellent depiction of sexuality generally, the central focus is on Casanova himself, his aging and loss of power. Women are there as ways of offering dramatic opportunities to demonstrate the disintegration of the hero. At least for me (and it has been some time since I viewed the film), the most memorable female is, in fact, the mechanical one given to Casanova for his entertainment.

But in *City of Women*, which shares a somewhat similar interest in the failing power and aging of the protagonist, something seems to have changed. Women themselves cease to be backdrops against which the course of a hero is presented. Instead, collectively, they are seen as a force which he must now acknowledge. In the presence of their reality (Donatella as guerrilla), the insubstantial dream collapses and the dreamer awakes.

To the extent that we identify Fellini with Snaporaz, to such a degree might we see the creator having made the same discovery as his hero. The role of Mastroianni then becomes crucial, for he is the link between the director and the character. Many critics assume that Mastroianni is, in fact, Fellini's alter ego, a fact which Fellini does not deny but which he qualifies by saying that *everything* in a film is his alter ego.[8] Even if we do not make an absolute identification, though, we still have a remarkable film in which, for the first time as far as I can tell, Fellini presents a truly new view of women.

NOTES

[1] Richard Schickel, "Garage Sale," *Time* April 20, 1982: 84; John Simon, "Diplomatic Immunity," *The National Review* 33 (June 26, 1981): 734.

[2] Diane Jacobs, "Fellini and Women," *Horizon* May 1981: 70; Molly Haskell, "The Maestro Mocks Himself: Fellini and Feminism," *The Village Voice* 25 (June 23, 1980): 43; Marie Jean Lederman, "Dreams and Vision in Fellini's *City of Women*," *Journal of Popular Film and Television* 9, 3 (1981): 114–22.

[3] Gideon Bachmann, "Federico Fellini: The Cinema Seen as a Woman. . . ," *Film Quarterly* 34, 2 (1980–81): 8.

[4] V. F. Perkins, "Film as Film," in *Film Theory and Criticism,* 2nd ed., eds. Gerald Mast and Marshall Cohen (New York: Oxford, 1979) 53.

[5] Lev Kuleshov, *Kuleshov on Film*, ed. Ronald Levaco (Berkeley: University of California Press, 1974) 53.

[6] Bachmann, 8.

[7] Laura Mulvey, "Visual Pleasure and Narrative Cinema," *Screen* 16, 3 (1975): 10.

[8] William Wolf, "Fellini and Mastroianni: Meeting of the Minds," *New York* (April 6, 1981): 61.

13. DECONSTRUCTED MEANING IN TWO SHORT STORIES BY FLANNERY O'CONNOR

Mary Jane Schenck

MANY CONTEMPORARY THEORIES of criticism address problems of meaning based on philosophies of language and the aesthetics of reception, so we worry less today about the author's conscious intentions than in previous times. Nevertheless, interpreting works of an author who has commented extensively on his or her own art may still be considered presumptuous. When the author has offered religious interpretations, counterarguments may seem to border on the heretical. Such are the risks for critics attempting to discuss how the fiction of Flannery O'Connor creates meanings in addition to or in contrast with what she herself said about her work.

O'Connor frequently commented on the Catholic faith, which she insisted formed her work, and most critics accept her own exegetical interpretations of her bizarre and troubling stories. Although the stories seem too brutal to be illustrations of Christian doctrine, at least as we conventionally conceive of it, O'Connor was able to justify her preoccupation with the ugly and grotesque by insisting on the writer's role as a prophet who must shake the reader and open his complacent eyes to reality and the need for grace. She was quite emphatic about the didactic function of the narrated events for both characters and readers, though the complications of interpreting her stories arise from the fact that they are not straightforward narratives like parables or exempla. Her texts are thoroughly ironic, and her use of irony creates ambiguities that undercut her own interpretations, even suggesting opposite ones, as other critics have suggested.[1]

What I would like to do is consider the ironic language of the texts in light of what Baudelaire in "De l'Essence du Rire" and Paul de Man in "The Rhetoric of Temporality" have revealed about this figure. For Baudelaire, comedy results from a doubling of spectator and laughable object or person. The heightened form of comedy, called irony, is in part an internalized doubling; it is a capacity to be at once self and other. As de Man explains:

> The *dedoublement* thus designates the activity of a consciousness by which a man differentiates himself from the non-human world. . . . The reflective disjunction not only occurs *by means of* language as a privileged category, but it transfers the self out of the empirical world into a world constituted out of, and in, language. . . . Language thus conceived divides the subject into an empirical self, immersed in the wold, and a self that becomes like a sign in its attempt at differentiation and self-definition.[2]

What de Man says of the ironic consciousness accurately depicts the method by which characters are created and create themselves in O'Connor's fiction. In "A Good Man is Hard to Find" and "The River," characters consciously or unconsciously use both written and oral language as well as pictorial "texts" to create a doubled self to escape an empirical one. To the extent that they succeed, they illustrate the performative quality of language, momentarily creating reality rather than reflecting it. But most of O'Connor's characters fail to understand the performative and arbitrary nature of their language. The disastrous climaxes so characteristic of her fiction are created in part by the conflict between the two selves as well as the conflict between characters who all may be doubled. The ironic doubling leads to a complete disintegration of the self at the moment when the character must confront the absence of grounding behind the linguistic self. As de Man explains, this process is not a finite or affirmative one. It is a radical process of deconstruction leading to madness. In a statement that well could have been written about the ironic process in O'Connor's fiction, de Man says:

> Irony is unrelieved *vertige,* dizziness to the point of
> madness. Sanity can exist only because we are wil-
> ling to function within the conventions of duplicity
> and dissimulation, just as social language dissimu-
> lates the inherent violence of relationships among
> human beings. Once this mask is shown to be a
> mask, the authentic being underneath appears neces-
> sarily as on the verge of madness.[3]

As we will see in the following discussion, the unmasking of language in O'Connor's stories leads very precisely to violence, if not
madness.

"A Good Man is Hard to Find" presents a masterful portrait of
a woman who creates a self and a world through language. From the
outset, the grandmother relies on "texts" to structure her reality. The
newspaper articles about The Misfit mentioned in the opening paragraph of the story is a written text which has a particular status in the
narrative. It refers to events outside and prior to the primary *récit,*
but it stands as an unrecognized prophecy of the events which occur
at the end. For Bailey, the newspaper story is not important or
meaningful, and for the grandmother it does not represent a real
threat but is part of a ploy to get her own way. It is thus the first one
of her "fictions," one which ironically comes true. The grandmother's whole personality is built upon the fictions she tells herself and
her family. Although she knows Bailey would object if she brought
her cat on the trip, the grandmother sneaks the cat into the car, justi-
fying her behavior by imagining, "he would miss her too much and
she was afraid he might brush against one of the gas burners and
accidently asphyxiate himself."[4] She also carefully cultivates a fiction about the past when people were good and when "children were
more respectful of their native states and their parents and everything
else" (119). As she tells Red Sam at the Tower when they stop to
eat, "People are certainly not nice like they used to be" (122).

The grandmother reads fictional stories to the children, tells
them ostensibly true stories, and provides a continual gloss on the
physical world they are passing. "Little niggers in the country don't
have things like we do. If I could paint, I'd paint that picture" (122).
Lacking that skill, the grandmother nevertheless verbally "creates" a
whole universe as they ride along. "'Look at the graveyard!' the
grandmother said, pointing it out. 'That was the old family burying

127

ground. That belonged to the plantation'" (120). She creates the stories behind the visual phenomena she sees and explains relationships between events or her own actions which have no logic other than that which she lends them.

Her most important fiction is, of course, the story of the old plantation house which becomes more of an imperative as she tells it. The more she talks about it, the more she wants to see it again, so she does not hesitate to self-consciously lie about it. "'There was a secret panel in this house,' she said craftily, not telling the truth but wishing she were . . ." (123). At this point we see clearly the performative quality of the grandmother's language. At first it motivates her own desire, then spills over onto the children, finally culminating in their violent outburst of screaming and kicking to get their father to stop the car. The performative quality of her language becomes even more crucial when she realizes that she has fantasized the location of the house. She does not admit it, but her thoughts manifest themselves physically: "The thought was so embarrassing that she turned red in the face and her eyes dilated and her feet jumped up, upsetting her valise in the corner" (124). Of course, it is her physical action which frees the cat and causes the accident. After the accident, she again fictionalizes about her condition, hoping she is injured so she can deflect Bailey's anger, and she cannot even manage to tell the truth about the details of the accident.

The scene with The Misfit is the apogee of the grandmother's use of "fictions" to explain and control reality, attempts that are thwarted by her encounter with a character who understands there is no reality behind her words. When the grandmother recognizes The Misfit, he tells her it would have been better if she hadn't, but she has *named* him, thus forcing him to become what is behind his self-selected name. In a desperate attempt to cope with the threat posed by the murderer, the grandmother runs through her litany of convenient fictions. She believes that there are class distinctions ("I know you're a good man. You don't look a bit like you have common blood" [127]), that appearance reflects reality ("You shouldn't call yourself The Misfit because I know you're a good man at heart. I can just look at you and tell" [128]), that redemption can be achieved through work ("You could be honest too if you'd only try. . . .Think how wonderful it would be to settle down . . ." [129]), and finally, that prayer will change him ("'Pray, pray,' she commanded him" [130]).

In contrast to the grandmother, whose flood of questions, explanations, and exhortations accompany the sequence of murderous events, the mother and Bailey react only physically. Deprived of language, they are barely more than props in the drama unfolding around them. Even the grandmother soon starts to lose her voice, the only mechanism that stands between her and reality. When she does try to tell The Misfit he must pray, her language has become fractured; all that comes out is the end of a sentence. "She wanted to tell him that he must pray. She opened and closed her mouth several times before anything came out. Finally she found herself saying, 'Jesus, Jesus,' meaning, Jesus will help you, but the way she was saying it, it sounded as if she might be cursing" (131). She finally loses control of her language and the myths they provide: "'Maybe He didn't raise the dead,' the old lady mumbled, not knowing what she was saying and feeling so dizzy that she sank down in the ditch with her legs twisted under her" (132).

When she reaches out to touch The Misfit and says, "Why you're one of my babies. You're one of my own children" (132), she either has uttered her final fantasy, having lost touch with reality as she confuses The Misfit (who is now wearing Bailey's shirt) with her own child, or she is attempting a last ingratiating appeal for his sympathies. O'Connor's interpretation of this line is that at this moment the grandmother realizes, "even in her limited way, that she is responsible for the man before her and joined to him by ties of kinship which have their roots deep in the mystery she has been merely prattling about so far."[5] This is one possible reading of the scene and in some quarters the accepted one, but we could also say that the grandmother simply is wrong again, and her comment provokes The Misfit into shooting her. Surely we witness here the moment when a clash of language creates the vertiginous movement of irony into violence and madness. The Misfit rejects her interpretations of his being and refuses to provide a grounding for that language. Her fictions are proven to be "just talk" and both her empirical and linguistic self are destoyed.

In counterpoint to the grandmother's slow destruction as each verbal system she has created fails to reflect the reality around her, The Misfit uses language literally to relate events, at the same time recognizing the dangerous power of words. His language accurately describes the accident scene: "'We turned over twice!' said the grandmother. 'Oncet,' he corrected. 'We seen it happen'" (126). He is the only one who seems to know that sometimes language fails utterly: "He seemed to be embarassed as if he couldn't think of anything to say" (127).

His understanding of himself is grounded not in a knowledge of the events of his empirical self but in the recognition that language has created him. His father provided him an essence by describing him as "a different breed of dog." He knows that he has been or done various things in his life, but he is curiously unclear about the crime which sent him to jail. Nevertheless, he says his punishment is no mistake for two reasons—a written document says he committed it and a psychiatrist told him so. Even though he maintains it was a lie, he accepts the power of words to define his existence, and he knows that he should get things in writing in order to control his life. Since he cannot make sense of the events of his empirical self, he quite consciously creates a double by renaming himself The Misfit and living out its violent implications. The phenomenon of a character acquiring a new identity by using a new name is common to both stories we are discussing, and it is the most explicit indication of the linguistically doubled self so crucial to the irony of the texts.

We might believe that The Misfit through his ironic vision has at least created a self that copes with the empirical world when he says, "It's nothing for you to do but enjoy the few minutes you got left the best way you can—by killing somebody or burning down his house or doing some other meanness to him. No pleasure but meanness" (132). But in the very last line of the story, he deconstructs even this doubled self: " 'Shut up, Bobby Lee,' The Misfit said. 'It's no real pleasure in life'" (133). His strange alternations between polite talk and cold-blooded murder and his last statement demonstrate the radical shifting back and forth between selves that cancel each other figuratively as he has literally cancelled the shifting consciousness of the grandmother.

In "The River," a small child is taken out for the day by a baby-sitter who unwittingly provides him with the "texts" that he will use to double himself and escape from the reality of an existence with parents who party, tell lots of jokes, and neglect him both emotionally and physically. As we see him at the beginning, his empirical self is passive and nonverbal: "He had a long face and bulging chin and half-shut eyes set far apart. He seemed mute and patient, like an old sheep waiting to be let out" (158). As he and his baby-sitter, Mrs. Connin, wait for the bus, she asks his name. "His name was Harry Ashfield and he had never thought at any time before of changing it. 'Bevel,' he said" (159). The doubled self is created almost spontaneously by adopting the name of a preacher Mrs. Connin has said would pray for his sick mother. The transformation is immediate, for in so naming himself, he allows Mrs. Connin to see him from a completely different perspective. " 'Why ain't that a coincident! . . . she stood looking at him as if he had become a marvel to her' " (159). From this point on, the child is referred to by Mrs. Connin and the narrator as Bevel.

On the streetcar ride, Bevel reveals his other, more duplicitous self. Mrs. Connin loans him a handkerchief, but when she falls asleep he sneaks it into the innerlining of his jacket, as he later does with the book of Bible stories. He seems to want to incorporate meaningful or attractive objects into a very empty empirical self by placing them close to his body.

Bevel builds his doubled self mainly through several "texts" related to the Christian story. The first one is the name of the preacher, and the second is Mrs. Connin's comments about the picture of Jesus. Later Bevel reflects on how much better she is than other sitters: "He had found out already this morning that he had been made by a carpenter named Jesus Christ. Before he had thought it had been a doctor named Sladewall, a fat man with a yellow mustache who gave him shots and thought his name was Herbert, but this must have been a joke. They joked a lot where he lived" (163). In this passage we see Bevel confronting the fact that events have different interpretations based on who is telling the story. He has had a problem knowing "what to believe" because of the jokes told in his family; in other words, an ironic form of language has already clearly left him with the *malaise* which comes from never being sure what is meant. Uncomfortable with the ironic language of his home, he clearly is happy to find a new interpretation of his birth.

When Mrs. Connin discovers that he doesn't know Jesus, she brings out *The Life of Jesus Christ for Readers Under Twelve,* thus introducing him to the third textual experience. Having been frightened earlier in the day by a hog, Bevel is especially taken by the picture of Jesus driving a crowd of pigs out of a man. Bevel sneaks the book into his inside pocket, and it seems to cause a change in him. In spite of the frightening events in Mrs. Connin's yard, he is now "dreamy and serene as they walked along . . ." (163).

The sermon by The Reverend Bevel Summers provides him with yet another textual experience that will give meaning and shape to the second self. The visual images he has of Jesus, the preacher's exciting talk of a river of pain that moves toward the Kingdom of Christ, and the promises of escape from trouble combine to move him further and further away from the ugly empirical reality symbolized by Mr. Paradise's purple tumor and debunking talk which cause him to hide in the folds of Mrs. Connin's dress.

The transformation of Harry Ashfield into Bevel is completed in the scene of his baptism. When Mrs. Connin points him out to the preacher, the previously passive, non-verbal child self-confidently proclaims his new identity before the crowd. "There were some rumors and Bevel turned and grinned over her shoulder at the faces looking at him. 'Bevel,' he said in a loud jaunty voice" (167). So the child is baptized as Bevel; the second self is legitimized through ritual.

After immersion he is no longer the serene grinning boy he had been, and we must wonder whether he is disappointed yet again at the failure of language to be true. He has not gotten to the Kingdom of Christ as promised by the preacher, and so he strikes out by unmasking the language of Mrs. Connin, who has asked the preacher to pray for his mother. "'Is she in pain?' the preacher asked. The child stared at him. 'She hasn't got up yet,' he said in a high dazed voice. 'She has a hangover'" (168). The preacher is angered by this revelation, perhaps because he, like Harry, is afraid he has been caught in a joke.

The doubled self cannot be sustained when Bevel returns home. As Mrs. Connin brings him in, "One of Bevel's eyes was closed and the other half closed; his nose was running and he kept his mouth open and breathed through it. The damp plain coat dragged down on one side" (169). He is the sheep being led to slaughter again, and the destruction is not long in coming. His mother greets him by his real name, and Mrs. Connin leaves in disgust, having been disabused about Harry/Bevel. When his mother discovers the Bible stories, another part of the doubled self is quickly demythologized when the adults snatch the book and laugh at the pictures, reducing it to its commercial value.

The next morning, as he wanders through the apartment strewn with the remains of another party, he methodically dumps the ashtrays and rubs the ashes into the rug, symbolically annihilating his empirical Ashfield self. Then, driven by a vision, he returns to the river and wades in, oblivious to the threat posed by Mr. Paradise. After several unsuccessful attempts to baptize himself and reach the Kingdom of Christ under the river, Bevel thinks:

> The river wouldn't have him. He tried again and came up choking. This was the way it had been when the preacher held him under. He had had to fight with something that pushed him back in the face. He stopped and thought suddenly: it's another joke, it's just another joke! He thought how far he had come for nothing and he began to hit and splash and kick the filthy river. (173)

His fury at the thought of being confined to his empirical self only leaves him as he feels the "gentle hand" of the current take him under.

The river was not a joke; it ultimately did accept him, and the audience can see that it all was a monstrous joke. The river takes the empirical self, destroying both consciousnesses. Only O'Connor's *belief* in the Catholic doctrine of the innocence of children can turn this story into one of salvation, and that belief is surely not shared by all readers. Even believers might question Harry's innocence. He lies, steals, and seems to be the "old man" he is called by some of the adults. In this respect, he resembles most O'Connor characters who see themselves as superior to their surroundings, but ultimately dupe themselves by creating a new identity based on a false understanding of language. He is as benighted by language as the grandmother, and the natural universe destroys him.

At the conclusion of both stories, the reader is left with a vision of destruction of human life both literal and figurative that is absurd rather than tragic because the victims are not heroic figures reduced to misfortune. They are ordinary, even unsympathetic characters who meet a grotesque fate. But they are not villains either, so it is difficult to accept the outcome as justified in any way by their conduct, no matter how much we may dislike the grandmother and the odd, aloof man-child, Bevel.

The difficulty in "reconstructing meaning," to use Wayne Booth's term, is that the central characters with whom we should

133

identify or from whom we hope to grasp some sense of meaning dissolve before our eyes into non-beings. The frightening moment occurs when we witness the fictional self confront a challenge to the reality of that self. As de Man and Baudelaire have pointed out:

> The movement of the ironic consciousness is anything but reassuring. The moment the innocence or authenticity of our sense of being in the world is put into question, a far from harmless process gets underway. It may start as a casual bit of play with a stray loose end of the fabric, but bejore long the entire texture of the self is unraveled and comes apart.[6]

The personalities of these characters are created by language, and this language fails them in one of two circumstances. They either are confronted by the natural world whose laws mock their interpretations, or they are confronted by a character who understands that language is mere convention. If the conventions are not shared, the encounter will lead to devastating physical or emotional violence. Seen from this perspective, the events which may seem absurd at first now appear to be well motivated by language. All types of language—names, Bible stories, daydreams, myths, sermons, and newspaper articles—function to create characters and events. The people are separated from each other and their world through this language, but at the outset the alienation is merely a tension inhibiting communication. By the end, when the language of the doubled selves has been unmasked, the characters behind it are totally deconstructed and no longer exist. Kierkegaard refers to "the infinite elasticity of irony, the secret trap door through which one is suddenly hurled downward, not like the schoolmaster in *The Elfs* who falls a thousand fathoms, but into the infinite nothingness of irony."[7] In spite of her intentions to the contrary, at the end of O'Connor's stories we feel a sudden shock of recognition as we witness the unraveling of the characters' personalities. Like the characters' fictional selves, our own experience with the text is deconstructed as we sense ourselves "fall through the trap door," uncertain of where, or if, we will land on any firm ground of meaning.

NOTES

[1] Josephine Hendin, *The World of Flannery O'Connor* (Bloomington: Indiana University Press, 1970); Gilbert Muller, *Nightmares and Visions: Flannery O'Connor and the Catholic Grotesque* (Athens: University of Georgia Press, 1972); Dorothy Walters, *Flannery O'Connor* (New York: Twayne Publishers, Inc., 1973).

[2] Paul de Man, "The Rhetoric of Temporality," *Interpretation: Theory and Practice*, ed. C.S. Singleton (Baltimore: Johns Hopkins Press, 1969) 195–96.

[3] de Man, 198.

[4] Flannery O'Connor, "A Good Man is Hard to Find," *The Complete Stories* (New York: Farrar, Straus, and Giroux, 1971) 118. Unless otherwise stated, subsequent excerpts are quoted from this source.

[5] Dorothy T. McFarland, *Flannery O'Connor, Modern Literature Monographs* (New York: Ungar, 1976) 21–22.

[6] de Man, 197.

[7] Søren Kierkegaard, *The Concept of Irony*, trans. Lee Cappel (Bloomington: University of Indiana Press, 1965) 63.

INDEX

Abrams, M. H., 86
Albertus Magnus, 29
alienation effect, 66, 71
allegory, 69, 71ff., 97
Alter, Robert, 101
ambiguity 1–9 *passim*; aesthetics of, 4; ethics of, 2, 3, 4. See author, character, clues, deconstruction, doubling, dream and film, episodes, existentialism, fiction and nonfiction, genre, imagination and stupidity, interpretation (levels of), irony, melodrama and distanciation, memory and metaphor, space and time, structural principle
Appel, Alfred, Jr., 103
archetypes, 11, 13; archetypal images, 12
Arendt, Hannah, 71
author, mixed codes with text and self, 104–116 *passim*

Bachelard, Gaston, 15
Bachmann, Gideon, 124
Barthes, Roland, 97–98
Baudelaire, Charles, 126, 134
Beauvoir, Simone de, 2–3
Belsey, Catherine, 115,
Benjamin, Walter, 66
Bergson, Henri, 44
Black, Max, 29
Bloom, Harold, 89
Boncompagno da Signa, 29
Booth, Wayne, 23, 28, 133–34
Bowers, Fredson, 88

Brandt, Willi, 73
Brecht, Bertolt, 65–66, 67, 71, 72, 114; didacticism of, 68; *Mother Courage,* 74
Brown, John Russel, 88
Buntline, Ned, 105–06, 110, 111, 112

Calderwood, James L., 92
Camus, Albert, 64
Caughie, John, 113
character, ambiguities of, 56–64 *passim*, 76–94 *passim*
Chatman, Seymour, 104
Christie, Agatha, 54
clues, with conflicting connotations, 99ff.
Conrad, Joseph, 60, 64
Cornford, Francis M., 44
Croft, Stephen, 86
Culler, Jonathan, 9, 86, 113, 114

Davidson, Donald, 23
deconstruction, 86, 111, 114; ambiguities with, 125–135 *passim*
demythologizing, 17, 109, 132
Derrida, Jacques, 86
Descartes (Cartesian), 12, 53
desire, staging of, 39ff.
Dessen, Alan C., 89, 90
Dickson, Hugh, 92
Dillard, Richard, 110
discontinuity, of narratives, 3; of ego, 111, 112
disjunction, of narrative structures, 3; of vision and script, 38; temporal, between plot and story, 35